T0340315

Disinformation and Manipulation in Digital Media

Drawing on research from multiple disciplines and international case studies, this book provides a comprehensive and up-to-date understanding of online disinformation and its potential countermeasures.

Disinformation and Manipulation in Digital Media presents a model of the disinformation process which incorporates four cross-cutting dimensions or themes: bad actors, platforms, audiences, and countermeasures. The dynamics of each dimension are analysed alongside a diverse range of international case studies drawn from different information domains including politics, health, and society. In elucidating the interrelationship between the four dimensions of online disinformation and their manifestation in different international contexts, the book demonstrates that online disinformation is a complex problem with multiple, overlapping causes and no easy solutions. The book's conclusion contextualises the problem of disinformation within broader social and political trends and discusses the relevance of radical innovations in democratic participation to counteract the post-truth environment.

This up-to-date and thorough analysis of the disinformation landscape will be of interest to students and scholars in the fields of journalism, communications, politics, and policy as well as policymakers, technologists, and media practitioners.

Eileen Culloty is a post-doctoral researcher at the DCU Institute for Future Media and Journalism where she leads research on countering disinformation as part of the H2020 project Provenance (grant no. 825227). Eileen sits on the management board of the Marie-Skłodowska-Curie European Training Network JOLT: Harnessing Digital and Data Technology for Journalism (grant no. 765140).

Jane Suiter is a political scientist with a focus on the public sphere and in particular on scaling up deliberation and disinformation. She has published in over 30 journals including *Science, International Journal of Political Science*, and the *International Journal of Communication* and is the author of two books including *Reimagining Democracy: Lessons in Deliberative Democracy from the Irish Frontline* (2019).

Routledge Focus on Communication and Society
Series Editor: James Curran

Routledge Focus on Communication and Society offers both established and early-career academics the flexibility to publish cutting-edge analysis on topical issues, research on new media or in-depth case studies within the broad field of media, communication and cultural studies. Its main concerns are whether the media empower or fail to empower popular forces in society; media organisations and public policy; and the political and social consequences of the media.

Bad News from Venezuela
Alan MacLeod

Reporting China on the Rise
Yuan Zeng

Alternative Right-Wing Media
Kristoffer Holt

Disinformation and Manipulation in Digital Media
Information Pathologies
Eileen Culloty and Jane Suiter

Disinformation and Manipulation in Digital Media

Information Pathologies

Eileen Culloty and Jane Suiter

Routledge
Taylor & Francis Group

LONDON AND NEW YORK

First published 2021
by Routledge
2 Park Square, Milton Park, Abingdon, Oxon OX14 4RN

and by Routledge
52 Vanderbilt Avenue, New York, NY 10017

Routledge is an imprint of the Taylor & Francis Group, an informa business

British Library Cataloguing-in-Publication Data
A catalogue record for this book is available from the British Library

Library of Congress Cataloging-in-Publication Data
Names: Culloty, Eileen, author. | Suiter, Jane, author.
Title: Disinformation and manipulation in digital media : information
pathologies / Eileen Culloty and Jane Suiter.
Description: Abingdon, Oxon ; New York, NY : Routledge, 2021. |
Series: Routledge focus on communication and society |
Includes bibliographical references and index.
Identifiers: LCCN 2020043526 (print) | LCCN 2020043527 (ebook)
Subjects: LCSH: Fake news–Social aspects. | Disinformation–Social aspects. |
Propaganda–Social aspects. | Digital media–Moral and ethical aspects. |
Internet–Moral and ethical aspects.
Classification: LCC PN4784.F27 .C85 2021 (print) |
LCC PN4784.F27 (ebook) | DDC 327.1/4–dc23
LC record available at https://lccn.loc.gov/2020043526
LC ebook record available at https://lccn.loc.gov/2020043527

ISBN: 978-0-367-51527-0 (hbk)
ISBN: 978-0-367-51525-6 (pbk)
ISBN: 978-1-003-05425-2 (ebk)

DOI: 10.4324/9781003054252

Typeset in Times New Roman
by Newgen Publishing UK

Contents

1   Introduction
Information pathologies

Across the world, all spheres of life have become subject to false information, conspiracy theories, and propaganda. These information pathologies are implicated in the global resurgence of vaccine preventable diseases, the subversion of national politics, and the amplification of social divisions. In 2018, the United Nations Human Rights Council cited Facebook as a 'determining' factor in the ethnic cleansing of Myanmar's Rohingya population. A year later, the Oxford Internet Institute found evidence of efforts to manipulate public opinion in 70 countries (Bradshaw and Howard 2019). More recently, the Covid-19 pandemic brought an onslaught of conflicting reports, hoaxes, and conspiracy theories. The World Health Organisation (WHO) called it an 'infodemic': an overabundance of accurate and inaccurate claims that left many people confused about what to believe. In this context, it is unsurprising that a sense of crisis has become entrenched among policymakers, scholars, technologists, and others (see Farkas and Schou 2019).

While the need to develop countermeasures for disinformation is urgent, it is also challenging on many fronts. First, there are significant conceptual difficulties surrounding definitions of the problem. Second, there are practical impediments to developing fair and consistent moderation principles for enormous volumes of online content. Third, any proposed restriction on freedom of expression is necessarily accompanied by legal, ethical, and democratic reservations. Fourth, communication technologies are constantly evolving, which makes it difficult to design countermeasures that will be effective for the future. Fifth, and perhaps most crucially, there are major gaps in our understanding of the problem owing to the nascency of the research area and the lack of access to the platforms' data. As a result, there is broad agreement that something needs to be done, but there is far less clarity about what that should be.

Undoubtedly, our current digital age is predisposed to a 'shock of the new' whereby digital media phenomena can seem more radical than they are because we untether them from their historical precedents. Taking a long view of human history, there is nothing new about disinformation. To take one example, 'The Protocols of the Elders of Zion' emerged from Russia in 1903 and, in the guise of a leaked document, appeared to reveal a Jewish plot for global domination. It gained international traction through the endorsement of major public figures, including the US industrialist Henry Ford, and through news media coverage and the distribution of pamphlets. As with disinformation generally, it is difficult to delineate the direct effects of the document, but two important lessons can be drawn from this case: successful disinformation amplifies existing prejudices and relies on structures of communication power and influence.

There is much to be gained by adopting a historical understanding of disinformation (see Cortada and Aspray 2019). Nevertheless, while cognisant of historical continuities, we argue that online disinformation represents a fundamental change. The affordances of digital platforms – with their design features, business models, and content policies – distinguish contemporary disinformation from its historical precursors. Digital media have unprecedented consequences in terms of the scale and speed at which disinformation is dispersed as well as the range of content types and platforms in which it is manifest. While the motivations that lie behind the production and consumption of disinformation may not have changed substantially over time, the rapid evolution of digital platforms have created new opportunities for bad actors while leaving regulators struggling to keep pace.

All this is predicated on the wider 'platformization' of economic, political, and social life (Plantin and Punathambekar 2019). Entire sectors have become institutionally dependent on the major online platforms. The news media is an important case in point. By dominating how people access information, the platforms became integral to news publishers' distribution strategies (Cornia and Sehl 2018). However, the relationship was fundamentally asymmetrical. News publishers were subject to unpredictable changes in platform policies, such as changes to recommendation algorithms, and were largely unable to monetise the content they created. Meanwhile the platforms, Google and Facebook in particular, came to dominate online advertising; largely thanks to their ability to collect data from users who enjoyed free access to content. As these conditions contributed to a dramatic decline in the news media's advertising revenue, finding ways to support high-quality journalism is a major consideration within the broader effort to counteract online disinformation.

Of course, the challenges faced by journalism are just one contributing factor to the proliferation of online disinformation. The key aim of this book is to provide an overarching context for understanding this multifaceted and evolving problem. In what follows, we present our model of the online disinformation process and its potential mitigation.

The components of online disinformation

Reduced to its basic constituents, online disinformation, when it is successful, is a process that involves different actors and consecutive stages (see Figure 1.1). We model online disinformation in terms of the bad actors who create and push manipulative content, the platforms that enable the distribution and promotion of this content, and the audiences who give it meaning and impact through their willingness to engage with it. Of course, any given scenario of online disinformation is more complex than this basic model suggests and we elucidate this complexity in the succeeding chapters by interrogating each component of the process. Nevertheless, we suggest the value of this model is that it allows us to simultaneously map and assess various countermeasures as efforts to intervene in different stages of the online disinformation process. In so doing, we emphasise the need for a multi-pronged approach and the concluding chapter takes this further to argue that countermeasures are likely to be ineffective unless they are accompanied by broader efforts to address deep-seated issues relating to public trust and democratic legitimacy.

The first stage in the process involves the so-called bad actors who create and push online disinformation. Bad actors may be defined collectively for their common intention to deceive or manipulate the public, but it is important to recognise that the nature of bad actors is multifarious. To date, much of the scholarly and journalistic attention

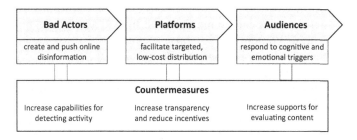

Figure 1.1 The online disinformation process

has focused on state-backed bad actors in the political domain; primarily on Russia's Internet Research Agency. As outlined in Chapter 2, we are also interested in the broader range of bad actors who are intent on misinforming the public or subverting public debate. A nuanced understanding of bad actors is complicated by the fact that much of what we know is derived from leaks and investigative journalism. Moreover, robust investigations – whether academic, journalistic, or parliamentary – have been hampered by a lack of useful data from the platforms (Boffey 2019). Nevertheless, we suggest that a broad understanding of bad actors may be derived by assessing: who they are or represent (e.g. states, corporations, social movements); their primary motivations (e.g. political, financial, ideological); and, of course, their tactics (e.g. creating deceptive content, influencing media agendas). The answers to these questions are typically inferred from the digital traces left online by bad actors; that is, by analysing disinformation content and how it has propagated through online networks. This brings us to the second component of our model – the platforms – as the strategies and tactics of bad actors take shape in line with the affordances of digital platforms.

The infrastructures of the platforms facilitate disinformation and incentivise low-quality content in many ways. As noted above, platform advertising models have had a detrimental impact on professional news. They also allow bad actors to monetise their disinformation. In addition, recommendation algorithms appear to have 'filter bubble effects' that amplify existing biases and potentially push people towards more extreme positions (Hussein et al. 2020). Recommendation algorithms aim to provide users with relevant content by grouping them according to their shared interests. This approach is relatively benign when those interests centre on sports and hobbies, but the implications are severe when those interests are defined by conspiracy theories and hate. More generally, the platforms' engagement metrics – likes, shares, and followers – incentivise attention-grabbing content including clickbait journalism and hoaxes. These metrics can be manipulated by bad actors who piggyback on trending content and use false accounts and automated bots to inflate the popularity of content (Shao et al. 2018).

Nevertheless, receptive audiences are arguably the most important component of the process. After all, disinformation only becomes a problem when it finds a receptive audience that is willing, for whatever reasons, to believe, endorse or share it. Understanding what makes audiences receptive to disinformation and in what circumstances is therefore crucial. Many researchers are trying to answer this question and what they find is a complex overlap of factors relating to biased reasoning and the triggering of negative emotions such as fear and anger. These tendencies are amplified on social media where our attention is perpetually distracted. Moreover, quite apart from any bias on the part of the individual, repeated exposure to disinformation can increase perceptions of credibility over time (De keersmaecker et al. 2020; Fazio et al. 2015). Thus, reducing exposure to disinformation and providing supports to help audiences evaluate content have been to the forefront of efforts to mitigate disinformation.

There are ongoing debates about how to counteract online disinformation without undermining freedom of expression. Since 2016, a wide range of technological, audience focused, and legal and regulatory interventions have been proposed (see Funke and Flamini 2020). Technological interventions aim to advance the ability to detect and monitor disinformation. For their part, the platforms have variously taken action to reduce the visibility of certain content, but face calls for more radical action to improve transparency and accountability. Within the media and educational sectors, there has been a rapid growth in verification and fact-checking services and a renewed focus on media and information literacy. Legal and regulatory interventions are perhaps the most controversial, ranging from new laws prohibiting the spread of false information to proposals for the regulation of the platforms. Authoritarian states and democratic states that are 'backsliding' into authoritarianism are both exploiting concerns about disinformation to silence critics and increase their control over the media. For example, Hungary recently introduced emergency Covid-19 measures that permit prison terms for publicising disinformation (Walker 2020). These and similar bills are widely criticised for their potentially chilling impact on freedom of expression and such cases accentuate the need for international leadership to protect fundamental rights and freedoms.

Conceptual approach

This book adopts an international and multi-disciplinary perspective on online disinformation and its mitigation. As a growing research area, important empirical insights are emerging from multiple disciplines including communication studies, computer science, cognitive science, information psychology, and policy studies. At the same time, technologists and investigative journalists are deepening our understanding of the problem and a range of actors are developing new initiatives and countermeasures. While grounded primarily in communication studies, we draw on developments in all of these areas to provide a comprehensive and up-to-date understanding of the disinformation environment.

Throughout the book, we utilise a selection of international case studies that represent different information domains including politics, health, and social relations. While there are valuable studies of disinformation within specific countries (primarily the US) and thematic areas (primarily politics), we present a wider perspective in order to elucidate the dynamics of the disinformation process. Context is vital. The architectures, interfaces, moderation mechanisms, and participatory behaviours of social media platforms are neither static nor universal (see Karpf 2019; Munger 2019). Rather, they are temporally situated and patterns of audience engagement are relative to their media, political, and social contexts. It follows that the dynamics of online disinformation are highly variable and understanding this variability is essential for assessing the threats and developing effective countermeasures. In elucidating the interrelationship between the four key components of the online disinformation process and their manifestation in different international contexts, we emphasise that online disinformation is a complex problem with multiple, overlapping causes and no easy solutions.

Throughout the book, we use the term online disinformation rather than the more popular term 'fake news'. The latter is a specific subset of disinformation and the term is already polluted through its invocation as a term of abuse for the news media. Nevertheless, we note that current definitions of the problem are broad, encompassing disinformation, 'fake news', manipulation, propaganda, fabrication, and satire (see Tandoc et al. 2018). In part, this definitional confusion is a consequence of the variety of forms and genres in which disinformation is manifest. It may appear as news articles, memes or tweets and its substantive content can range from the complete fabrication of facts to their distortion or decontextualisation (Wardle and Derakhshan 2017). We take the view that it is not necessarily helpful to think in strict terms of true and false or fake and real. Disinformation is often multi-layered containing a mix of verified, dubious, and false statements. Moreover, in many cases, the distinction between disinformation and ideological opinion may be difficult to define because 'political truth is never neutral, objective or absolute' (Coleman 2018: 157). Ultimately, we suggest the threat of disinformation has less to do with individual claims than the cumulative assault on trust and evidence-based deliberation.

Book outline

Following this introduction, successive chapters focus on each element of our disinformation process model: bad actors, platforms, audiences, and countermeasures. The second chapter examines the bad actors who produce and distribute disinformation. With a specific focus on disinformation about politics, climate change, and immigration, we examine different types of actors, their motivations, and the tactics through which they seek influence. Ultimately, we suggest that focusing on content (e.g. false claims) and behaviour (e.g. trolling) alone is insufficient for an understanding of how bad actors exercise influence on a society or culture. As a case study, we highlight India's disinformation crisis, which is notable for the range of actors involved and its online and offline dimensions.

The role of platforms in enabling bad actors is discussed in Chapter 3. To a large extent, we suggest that online disinformation is a consequence of platform business models and the absence of robust oversight mechanisms. We examine two major features of the platform's business models – algorithms and advertising – and assess the impact on the information environment including the destabilisation of quality journalism. We then consider governance proposals that aim to enhance transparency and accountability. Taking YouTube as a case study, we highlight how search and recommendation facilities subvert information seekers by promoting conspiracy theorists and extremist ideologies.

Chapter 4 examines what makes audiences susceptible, and potentially resilient, to online disinformation. A key aim of this chapter is to move beyond simplistic ideas of audience vulnerability. Drawing on research from cognitive psychology, political communication, and human-computer interaction, we present a more nuanced understanding of the complex overlap of factors that shape audience engagement with disinformation and, consequently, make it difficult to pin-point disinformation as a causal influence on audience attitudes and behaviour. Nevertheless, we may identify how bad actors, working within the affordances of platforms, are able to exploit audiences with emotionally manipulative content. In this regard, our case study highlights how the strategies employed by the anti-vaccine, or anti-vax, movement intersect with the factors known to increase audience receptivity to disinformation.

In light of the preceding chapters, Chapter 5 assesses the range of disinformation countermeasures that have been introduced or are in development across the world. We contextualise how various technological, audience-focused, and regulatory measures aim to intervene in the disinformation process by limiting the actions of bad actors, improving platform accountability, and providing support for audiences. However, these efforts are impeded by major gaps in our understanding of disinformation and its impacts. In particular, they are impeded by the platforms' reluctance to provide comprehensive data to third-party researchers. In this context, the implications of proposed countermeasures, including the potential for unintended consequences, needs close scrutiny. The European Union's multi-pronged action plan to counteract online disinformation is examined in the case study.

The concluding chapter on post-truth communication contextualises the proliferation of online disinformation in terms of wider concerns about public trust, truth, and democratic legitimacy. We examine how disinformation countermeasures can be embedded in more radical efforts to rethink democratic participation such as deliberative democracy. In so doing, we argue that it is a mistake to allow the proliferation of disinformation to overshadow the remarkable advances of digital communication. Despite all the flaws, it remains true that the internet and related technologies have been revolutionary in opening up access to information and providing opportunities for expression.

In his writings on media and democracy, the pragmatist philosopher Jurgen Habermas (1984, 2006) makes a crucial distinction between strategic actions that aim to control people and communicative actions that aim to advance mutual understanding and cooperation. Digital technologies have clearly created new ground for the latter, but infrastructure alone cannot guarantee communicative action. Put simply, the digital world requires governance, accountability, and transparency. As Habermas (2006: 420) argues, 'an inclusive civil society must empower citizens to participate in and respond to a public discourse which, in turn, must not degenerate into a colonising mode of communication'. The challenge then is to mitigate information pathologies while finding ways to advance understanding and cooperation.

References

Boffey D (2019) Facebook withholding data on its anti-disinformation efforts. *The Guardian*, 28 February. Available at: www.theguardian.com/technology/2019/feb/28/facebook-withholding-data-anti-disinformation-efforts-eu.

Bradshaw S and Howard P (2019) *The Global Disinformation Order: 2019 Global Inventory of Organised Social Media Manipulation*. Oxford: Oxford Internet Institute.

Coleman S (2018) The elusiveness of political truth: From the conceit of objectivity to intersubjective judgement. *European Journal of Communication* 33(2): 157–171. DOI: 10.1177/0267323118760319.

Cornia A and Sehl A (2018) *Private Sector News, Social Media Distribution, and Algorithm Change*. Oxford: Reuters Institute for the Study of Journalism.

Cortada JW and Aspray W (2019) *Fake News Nation: The Long History of Lies and Misinterpretations in America*. Lanham: Rowman & Littlefield.

De Keersmaecker J, Dunning D, Pennycook G et al. (2020) Investigating the robustness of the illusory truth effect across individual differences in cognitive ability, need for cognitive closure, and cognitive style. *Personality and Social Psychology Bulletin* 46(2): 204–215. DOI: 10.1177/0146167219853844.

Farkas J and Schou J (2019) *Post-Truth, Fake News and Democracy: Mapping the Politics of Falsehood*. Abingdon: Routledge.

Fazio LK, Brashier NM, Payne BK et al. (2015) Knowledge does not protect against illusory truth. *Journal of Experimental Psychology: General* 144(5): 993–1002. DOI: 10.1037/xge0000098.

Funke D and Flamini D (2020) A guide to anti-misinformation actions around the world. *Poynter*. Available at: www.poynter.org/ifcn/anti-misinformation-actions/.

Habermas J (1984) *The Theory of Communicative Action*. Boston: Beacon Press.

Habermas J (2006) Political communication in media society: does democracy still enjoy an epistemic dimension? The impact of normative theory on empirical research. *Communication Theory* 16(4): 411–426. DOI: 10.1111/j.1468-2885.2006.00280.x.

Hussein E, Juneja P and Mitra T (2020) Measuring misinformation in video search platforms: An audit study on YouTube. *Proceedings of the ACM on Human-Computer Interaction* 4(CSCW1): 1–27. DOI: 10.1145/3392854.

Karpf D (2020) Two provocations for the study of digital politics in time. *Journal of Information Technology & Politics* 17(2): 87–96. DOI: 10.1080/19331681.2019.1705222.

Munger K (2019) The limited value of non-replicable field experiments in contexts with low temporal validity. *Social Media + Society* 5(3). DOI: 10.1177/2056305119859294.

Plantin J-C and Punathambekar A (2019) Digital media infrastructures: pipes, platforms, and politics. *Media, Culture & Society* 41(2): 163–174. DOI: 10.1177/0163443718818376.

Shao C, Ciampaglia GL, Varol O et al. (2018) The spread of low-credibility content by social bots. *Nature Communications* 9(1): 4787. DOI: 10.1038/s41467-018-06930-7.

Tandoc EC, Lim ZW and Ling R (2018) Defining 'Fake News': A typology of scholarly definitions. *Digital Journalism* 6(2): 137–153. DOI: 10.1080/21670811.2017.1360143.

United Nations Human Rights Council (2018) *Report of the Independent International Fact-finding Mission on Myanmar*. 27 August. Geneva: United Nations Human Rights Council. Available at: www.ohchr.org/EN/HRBodies/HRC/MyanmarFFM/Pages/ReportoftheMyanmarFFM.aspx.

Walker S (2020) Hungary passes law that will let Orbán rule by decree. *The Guardian*, 30 March. Available at: www.theguardian.com/world/2020/mar/30/hungary-jail-for-coronavirus-misinformation-viktor-orban.

Wardle C and Derakhshan H (2017) *Information Disorder: Toward an Interdisciplinary Framework for Research and Policy Making*. DGI(2017)09. Brussels: Council of Europe.

2 Bad actors

Bad actors is a generic term for those who intentionally create and propagate disinformation. This category of actors is strikingly diverse – encompassing states, corporations, social movements, and individuals – and their motivations span a spectrum of political, ideological, and financial interests. They also vary considerably in terms of the audiences they target and the levels of coordination involved. Given this diversity, it is unsurprising that a new lexicon of competing terms has emerged to describe bad actors and their tactics. Here, we refer to bad actors as a catchall term for trolls, cyber troops, and related concepts. Whatever the preferred terminology, the core issue is to devise a means of identifying bad actors and a clear picture of the threats they pose. Much of what we know comes from piecemeal investigations by journalists, NGOs, academics, and public disclosures by the platforms. To a large extent, we understand bad actors through the digital traces they leave behind in public fora; that is, through their patterns of online behaviour and the content they create. Comparatively little is known about how bad actors operate in closed spaces such as WhatsApp and Facebook groups. Consequently, as with so many other aspects of disinformation, our understanding of bad actors is partial and incomplete.

To facilitate analysis, many authors have devised taxonomies of bad actors and their tactics (see for example Molina et al. 2019; Wardle and Derakhshan 2017). While enormously helpful, these taxonomies are challenged by the ever-changing nature of the environment. After all, bad actors are opportunistic in reacting to world events and their tactics evolve in response to countermeasures. Prior to Covid-19, concern centred on disinformation by state actors and the alarming prospect of 'deepfake' manipulations enabled by advances in artificial intelligence. Yet, in the initial months of Covid-19 the online environment was flooded with disinformation by non-state actors using 'cheapfakes' that required minimal skills and resources (Brennan et al. 2020). Of course, state actors also exploited the crisis and some of disinformation was highly sophisticated, but what Covid-19 underscored is the need to be vigilant about multiple actors and multiple kinds of manipulation.

To date, legislators have primarily focused on state actors and attempts to undermine democratic elections. The impact of disinformation on election outcomes is perhaps overstated (Karpf 2019). However, bad actors do not have to influence voting behaviour to be disruptive as disinformation campaigns can amplify social division, increase polarisation, and distort public debate. Beyond elections, a range of disinformation campaigns by non-state actors pose significant threats to society: corporations agitate against action on climate change, healthcare charlatans discourage vaccinations, and far-right extremists promote a nativist ideology that scapegoats minorities. These disinformation campaigns predate social media, but digital technologies have provided new ways to target audiences and new opportunities for transnational cooperation. Importantly, these campaigns encompass online and offline dimensions whereby disinformation is propagated through networks of media outlets, think-tanks, and online influencers.

In this context, this chapter examines the interplay between different kinds of bad actors including their motivations and tactics. While bad actors can produce disinformation about any topic imaginable, we focus in particular on three major themes: politics, climate change, and immigration. As a case study, we focus on India's disinformation crisis, which is entangled in pronounced social, political, and geo-political divisions. Based on this and similar cases, we suggest that bad actors and the threats they pose need to be understood within wider offline contexts and for their cumulative assault on the information environment.

Bad actors

Motivation is key to the designation of bad actors and, indeed, to the definition of disinformation as the intentional creation and distribution of false information. However, understanding motivation can be challenging as motives are generally inferred from content and behaviour. This creates a high burden of proof for identifying bad actors and gives rise to ambiguities; for example, between those who know disinformation is false and those who believe it is true. Individuals and organisations are motivated to create disinformation for a variety of reasons. In what follows, we outline three major interests: political, financial, and ideological. However, it is important to recognise that these categories are fluid. An individual bad actor may occupy multiple categories over time and the interests of different bad actors can intersect.

Political interests: While anyone can create disinformation, state actors have access to considerable financial and organisational resources. Of course, state-run propaganda campaigns are nothing new and 'information warfare' has long been a feature of military and intelligence operations. During the Cold War, Soviet intelligence agencies routinely conducted 'active measures' – including leaking false information, spreading false rumours, and creating forgeries – to advance Soviet influence and foreign policy goals. In the US, the practice of information warfare arguably reached a zenith in the mass surveillance operations uncovered in the 2000s. Meanwhile, China's 2003 'Three Warfares' doctrine enshrined the use of media manipulation as a tool for foreign policy (Iasiello 2016). In the process, information warfare has given way to the more encompassing concept of 'hybrid threats': that is, the blended deployment of diplomatic, military, economic, and technological strategies to advance state interests.

Just as social media changed the dynamics of international diplomacy (Seib 2016), they have also created new opportunities for state-backed disinformation. Such campaigns are typically covert operations that obscure the identity of those who engineer them – whether military and intelligence units or state-backed private companies such as Russia's Internet Research Agency (IRA). Consequently, state-run disinformation campaigns are difficult to detect (see Bradshaw and Howard 2019). To date, Facebook and Twitter have accused seven countries of operating foreign influence operations: China, India, Iran, Pakistan, Russia, Saudi Arabia, and Venezuela (ibid.). Regarding Russia specifically, researchers at Graphika have traced disinformation campaigns across seven languages and hundreds of online outlets (Nimmo et al. 2020).

The IRA's targeting of the US public prior to the 2016 presidential election is one of the most widely studied disinformation campaigns. Yet, while the resulting revelations intensified concerns about the integrity of elections worldwide, there is insufficient evidence to support the idea that disinformation is an effective tool for achieving foreign policy goals (Lanoszka 2019). The IRA campaign generated volumes of content and appeared to accumulate widespread engagement, but there is little reason to believe it had any influence on the election outcome. As David Karpf (2019) argues, 'generating social media interactions is easy; mobilising activists and persuading voters is hard'. Of course, the absence of direct impacts on voting behaviour does not mean the disinformation campaign was unsuccessful. Analyses have shown that IRA accounts sought to amplify social tensions; for example, by simultaneously supporting left-leaning and right-leaning positions and by exploiting the interests of African Americans in particular (Freelon and Lokot 2020).

Moreover, disinformation is not just a foreign policy tool. State actors may also be incentivised to use disinformation to control opinion among the domestic population. As outlined in the case study below, disinformation in India is partly driven by aggressive political campaigning (Mahapatra and Plagemann 2019). A 2019 analysis by the Oxford Internet Institute found evidence of disinformation campaigns targeting citizens in 70 countries (Bradshaw and Howard 2019). In each country, at least one political party or government agency used social media to influence the attitudes of the domestic public. Political disinformation is exacerbated by platform advertising and opportunities to microtarget personalised messages at segments of the online audience. This is an undemocratic practice for which there is little transparency on the part of the platforms that sell advertising or the political actors who buy it (ERGA 2020).

Financial interests: In the corporate world, the distinction between PR and disinformation is often dubious. Corporations are clearly incentivised to engage in disinformation when their financial interests are under threat. The template for corporate disinformation was established by the tobacco industry in its effort to suppress evidence for the dangers of smoking. Since the 1970s, fossil fuel companies have replicated the tobacco strategy to undermine climate science and delay policy action. This campaign is sustained by a network of media organisations and think-tanks funded by the tobacco and fossil fuel industries (Hope 2019). In particular, the Heartland Institute plays a central role in undermining climate science through the publication of pseudo-scientific reports, media appearances, and political lobbying (Boykoff and Farrell 2019).

For years, the news media have been complicit in this obfuscation of scientific evidence; principally by orchestrating artificial debates between climate scientists and climate-change denialists. Although news coverage has moved closer to the scientific consensus in many countries (Brüggemann and Engesser 2017), disinformation remains prevalent online. Moreover, there is a cultural alliance between corporate interests and the agendas of right-wing media as evidenced by the sustained attacks on Greta Thunberg, the teenage climate activist. Over time, the wide-ranging campaign against climate science has real public impact in terms of reducing support for climate action and exasperating political polarisation (Cook et al. 2017).

Financial interests also drive disinformation at the individual level. As outlined in Chapter 3, the ad-tech industry generates revenue for bad actors by driving traffic to websites that sell advertising. In particular, these bad actors are motivated to target the US public given the size of that market and the value of US advertising dollars. During the 2016 US presidential election, young people across the Balkans generated income in this way by targeting Trump voters. More recently, Facebook removed the Ukrainian-run 'I Love America' page, which accumulated one million followers by recycling posts featuring patriotic US-themes and cute animals (Papenfuss 2019). Taken collectively, the financial rewards are significant. The Global Disinformation Index (2019) estimates that advertising on disinformation websites generates some €200 million annually. In this context, it is perhaps unsurprising that Google reports a staggering daily volume of Covid-19 disinformation – 240 million messages – on its Gmail service (Murphy 2020).

Ideological interests: Ideological motivations are varied and often intersect with financial and political interests. This is evident in anti-vaccine disinformation (see Chapter 4) where a handful of well-financed organisations are responsible for the widespread promotion of anti-science disinformation. In other cases, ideological disinformation is driven by online subcultures. A network of misogynistic actors coordinate the online harassment of women (Ging 2019) and this anti-feminist ideology is implicated in violent attacks including mass shootings (Tomkinson, Harper, and Attwell 2020). Moreover, these misogynistic actors have a fluid relationship with the far-right subcultures that attack minorities (Marwick and Lewis 2017).

Worldwide, immigration is perhaps one of the most prevalent disinformation topics. Anti-immigrant disinformation is associated with a diverse range of actors including right-wing populists, far-right extremists, and alt-right influencers (Hope Not Hate 2019). In recent years, there is evidence of increased transnational cooperation among these actors (Avaaz 2019; Davey and Ebner 2017). For example, transnational actors mobilised against the 2018 Global Compact for Safe, Orderly and Regular Migration (GCM) and were responsible for almost half of the most popular YouTube videos on the topic (Institute for Strategic Dialogue 2019). Their core claim falsely asserted that the UN would compel states to outlaw criticism of immigration.

More generally, Islamophobia is the 'transnational glue' of far-right disinformation (Froio and Ganesh 2018: 19). In many countries, this rhetoric is normalised by political elites (Crandall et al. 2018) and often in compliance with national media outlets. In Hungary, prime minister Viktor Orbán regularly assails immigrants and his efforts are aided by the government's growing control over media outlets (Bajomi-Lázár 2019). This illiberal swerve is replicated across other democratic states (see Applebaum 2020). Much like the campaign against climate change, the condition that fuels anti-immigrant attitudes underscores the importance of viewing disinformation across its online and offline contexts.

Finally, it is important to consider the role of the amplifiers – media pundits, politicians, celebrities, and online influencers – who help popularise disinformation. Importantly, these actors do not have to endorse disinformation to be complicit in its propagation. Mainstream news media is complicit when it gives coverage to outlandish claims such as Donald Trump's conspiracy theory about the birthplace of Barack Obama (Rosenberg 2011). Amplifiers can remain at a remove from the creation of disinformation while acting as a bridge between extremism and acceptability. For example, Hartzell (2018: 8) characterises the alt-right as the 'youthful, intellectual, pro-white' faction of the far-right, which acts as a gateway between 'mainstream public discourse and white nationalism'. Overall, the diversity of the bad actors and amplifiers creates multiple points of exposure for audiences and different rhetorical strategies and tactics through which disinformation is packaged. In the process, disinformation travels from the fringe to the mainstream and there is a cumulative assault on the grounds for informed debate.

Manipulation tactics

The infrastructure of online platforms facilitates disinformation in many ways (see Chapter 3). As there is insufficient scope to discuss the intricacies of disinformation tactics in detail (see Paris and Donovan 2019; Wardle and Derakhshan 2017), we focus on two overarching features: the capacity to create virtual fakes and the capacity to influence agendas across the media system.

Virtual fakes: Concerns about authenticity have been prevalent since the early days of the web as was memorably encapsulated by Peter Steiner's 1993 cartoon caption: 'on the Internet, no one knows you're a dog'. While anonymity has important ethical and democratic functions (Asenbaum 2018), fake accounts also erode trust in online communication. Initially, social media seemed to bring an end to the Peter Steiner era of web anonymity, but social media platforms are plagued by fake accounts. In the first nine months of 2019, Facebook removed 5.4 billion fake accounts (Fung and Garcia 2019). On Twitter, an analysis of 200 million tweets about Covid-19 found that almost half had the characteristics of automated bots (Young 2020); although it should be noted that the identification of bots is prone to error (Gorwa and Guilbeault 2020).

Fake accounts and bots can be used to manipulate trends, promote disinformation stories, and present the illusion of grassroots support (Shao et al. 2018). For example, trending Twitter topics are hijacked to piggyback on popular content and push agendas (Graham 2016; Siapera et al. 2018). While such campaigns tend to be short lived, they have a 'liminal' power to disorientate public debate (Siapera et al. 2018). In contrast to paid advertising, content created by seemingly ordinary people tends to be perceived as more authentic and so is more persuasive (Lou and Yuan 2019). Bad actors exploit this to engage unsuspecting audiences. Ahead of the 2019 European Parliament elections, Avaaz (2019) uncovered a network of fake accounts operated by the far-right. Apart from inflating content through comments, likes, and shares, they built up audiences through the 'bait and switch' branding of Facebook pages. Pages were initially established around lifestyle interests like music and then switched to extremist content. Similar tactics are associated with the IRA including the impersonation of activist groups (Freelon and Lokot 2020).

All this is possible because online media flatten distinctions between different kinds of content and different kinds of content producer. Consequently, it is relatively easy to mimic the visual cues that designate an activist account or a trusted authority. At a basic level, bad actors create 'imposter' sources by replicating the logos and branding of organisations such as the WHO and the BBC (Wardle and Derakhshan 2017). More advanced manipulations create entire networks of fake expertise. *The Daily Beast* uncovered a network of fake experts who published more than 90 opinion articles in conservative media outlets including the *Washington Examiner*, *The Jerusalem Post*, and the *South China Morning Post* (Rawnsley 2020). The authors – supporting the policies of the United Arab Emirates – posed as political consultants and freelance journalists by using stolen or synthetic photos in their social media profiles, by claiming to have professional credentials in their LinkedIn accounts, and by cross-referencing each other's work to give the appearance of credibility.

Of course, false claims to expertise are nothing new and, in essence, they represent an old rhetorical strategy: the appeal to authority. Disinformation about climate change has frequently employed this tactic even though, paradoxically, climate deniers simultaneously dismiss the authority of climate science (Cook 2019). In the late 1990s, a 'global warning petition' emerged in which '30,000 scientists' appeared to reject the evidence for human-caused climate change. However, only 39 of the listed signatories had a relevant scientific qualification. Decades later, this petition resurfaced to become one of the most popular social media stories about climate change in 2016 (Readfearn 2016). This capacity to create fake personas and to unmoor content from its original context of production calls to mind Mike Sandbothe's (1998) characterisation of online communication as 'a consciously constructed and aesthetically staged artefact'. When everything online is reduced to textual cues, traditional distinctions between appearance and reality collapse. Deepfakes exemplify this more than any other type of disinformation. It is now possible to generate entirely synthetic images of people and to mimic the facial expressions and speech of real people. For a detailed account of audio-visual manipulation tactics and their historical contexts see Paris and Donovan (2019). Nevertheless, individual fakes only go so far. Sophisticated disinformation campaigns exploit the wider media system and they seek influence by engaging multiple tactics aimed at different platforms and audiences.

Exploiting the media system: As noted above, bad actors can launder disinformation through a web of outlets and amplifiers. Marwick and Lewis (2017: 30) describe this process as 'trading up the chain'. Disinformation narratives are formulated on lesser known platforms such as 4chan or Gab and are then circulated by sympathetic YouTube channels, Twitter influencers, and partisan media. In this way, disinformation is networked through successive sources and circular references to the same story give the appearance of legitimacy. Moreover, prominent individuals within the disinformation ecosystem can cite these sources without making any false claims themselves (Evans 2020). As these disinformation stories gain traction within online and partisan communities, they gain visibility and push towards the mainstream news media. In the US context, researchers have found that bad actors are intricately entwined with partisan media outlets and influence coverage of a range of topics from economics to international relations (Vargo, Guo, and Amazeen 2018).

Mainstream news media are also complicit in the promotion of disinformation by giving undue coverage to outlandish claims (Rosenberg 2011; Wells et al. 2016). From the bad actor's perspective, 'it doesn't matter if the media is reporting on a story in order to debunk or dismiss it; the important thing is getting it covered in the first place' (Marwick and Lewis 2017: 39) While platforms are rightly criticised for prioritising low-quality content through their engagement metrics and recommendation algorithms, mainstream news media must also bear responsibility for sensationalist coverage. Whether through carelessness, a lack of awareness, or a dearth of resources, the kind of journalistic failures exemplified by *The Daily Beast* investigation are entirely self-defeating for the news industry – particularly considering the widespread attack on the credibility of professional journalism as 'fake news'.

Any discussion of disinformation tactics can seem remote and Machiavellian. However, it is important to also consider the economic conditions that make disinformation work possible and even desirable. In some cases, conspiracy theorists and alt-right influences have turned themselves into profitable brands. For example, Alex Jones has amassed great personal wealth by peddling conspiracy theories and branded products (Warzel 2017). In other cases, efforts to exploit the media system form part of regular employment. Corporate and political actors pay trolls to counteract criticism and push agendas. This is an established practice in China where the '50 Cent Army' of paid (and voluntary) commentators spread pro-government messages across online forums. Insights into these practices are scarce. The 2018 US indictment of Internet Research Agency workers revealed that employees worked in shifts to manage several social media accounts and had targets for producing disinformation content (Barrett 2018). One of the most in depth studies comes from Ong and Cabañes' (2018: 14) analysis of the Philippines where paid trolling is a 'professionalised and normalised' industry. Crucially, the authors argue that this industry is 'dependent on the complicity of professional elites in advertising and PR as well as underpaid digital and creative workers' (ibid.). On this understanding, disinformation – at least in some cases – needs to be understood as a social and economic phenomenon in which there are hierarchies of bad actors and service workers.

Content and culture

To date, much of the popular discussion on disinformation or 'fake news' has focused on content. Proposed countermeasures, including media literacy and fact-checking, also place emphasis on the content of disinformation claims. However, focusing on content alone can obscure the operation of disinformation campaigns. In the case of far-right actors, the individual stories they publish may be factually accurate, but the campaign lies in the cumulative effect of endlessly repeating negative stories about immigrants and minorities. Moreover, by omitting key explanatory factors, adding textual amendments, or adopting different naming standards, a relatively neutral story can be transformed into one that is imbued with racist sentiment (Ekman 2019). In contrast to 'fake news' that is entirely fabricated, these disinformation stories contain nuggets of truth that are corroborated by mainstream news sources. This also poses a difficulty for fact-checkers because 'verifying the status of basic facts is one thing but questions about what facts mean and how they relate to reliable accounts of political reality cannot be reduced to the mechanics of automatic affirmation' (Coleman 2018:158). This is also clear in the case of climate change where the scientific facts are well established. What is absent, in some countries at least, is a social consensus. As such, disinformation about immigration and climate science are not necessarily about accepting or rejecting facts; they are drawn into a wider culture war about values and ideology.

In the Global North, and in the US in particular, a contemporary cultural war pits socially progressive ideas against conservatism and tradition. This affective polarisation is clearly a contributing factor for the spread of disinformation. For example, disinformation content often appeals to the existing biases of target audiences and is highly emotive in attempting to provoke outrage (Bakir and McStay 2018). In particular, disinformation plays on negative emotions such as fear, disgust, and anger (Paschen 2019). In this context, disinformation can play an important role in building and sustaining partisan communities. As social media status is conferred through the accumulation of followers and likes, users are incentivised to create content that will resonate among their peers and help them gain status within the community (Wardle and Derakhshan 2017). Among far-right actors, disinformation campaigns are a means of bolstering community cohesion and promoting anti-immigrant attitudes to the wider public (Ekman 2019). In such cases, the distinction between grassroots advocacy and professional trolling isn't always clear.

The participatory and highly visual nature of digital culture is central to these communities. Visual formats are effective vehicles for disinformation because visual information is processed more easily than text (Adaval et al. 2018). Moreover, it often falls outside content-based definitions of disinformation as false or misleading information. In 2016, Google removed a Chrome browser extension that automatically placed a 'visual echo' (i.e. triple parentheses) around certain names to identify them as Jewish (Plaugic 2016). Similarly, far-right actors make extensive use of memes, in-jokes, and irony to appeal to a broader, younger audience (Marwick and Lewis 2017). In the process, racism, Islamophobia, and misogyny are re-packaged in ambiguous ways that contribute to the gradual normalisation of previously unacceptable utterances (Ekman 2019). Thus, it becomes increasingly difficult to separate the propagation of visual disinformation from 'digital hate culture' (Ganesh 2018: 30).

Finally, we may consider the role of conspiracy theories, which have become a ubiquitous feature of contemporary culture. They are also a tool for state actors. During the protracted Syrian conflict, the Russian broadcaster RT claimed the Syrian opposition staged bombings to provoke US intervention (Yablokov 2015). These reports were well received by anti-imperialist activists who opposed intervention and by US conspiracy theorists who used the case to advance claims about the prevalence of 'crisis actors' in breaking news stories (Culloty 2020). This unlikely alliance of actors illustrates the fluid nature of conspiracy culture and the diverse motivations that can instigate endorsement of conspiracy claims.

Conspiracy theories often emerge in times of uncertainty when there is a demand for answers and a lack of consensus about the evidence. Unsurprisingly, Covid-19 brought conspiracy theories to the fore as people across the world struggled to make sense of what was happening. While sophisticated bad actors exploited the situation to advance an anti-vaccine agenda (see Cook et al. 2020), it appears that many ordinary people engaged with conspiracy theories without an intent to cause harm. Although conspiracy theories are often discussed in absolutist terms, there is a wide spectrum of endorsement between the 'true believers' and those who merely entertain the idea that a conspiracy theory might be true (Harambam 2020). Moreover, those who espouse conspiracy claims often see themselves as model citizens who are willing to think for themselves rather than blindly accept the authority of experts (ibid.).

Consequently, conspiracy theories feed into a culture of distrust while creating alternative communities that propagate disinformation. While it is easy to dismiss conspiracy theories as absurd, it is a mistake to assume that the substantive content matters more than the identities that are associated with conspiracy theory communities (Harambam 2020). As evidenced by Donald Trump's courting of the community surrounding the QAnon conspiracy theory (Zuckerman and McQuade 2019), bad actors are already attune to the power of these communities. Consequently, we suggest that efforts to counteract bad actors need to look beyond tactics and content to address the social and cultural dimensions that sustain communities of distrust.

Case study: disinformation in India

India, the world's largest democracy, is at the epicentre of information disorders, both within and outside its borders. India is a highly polarised country with stark inequalities and discriminatory practices towards its minority groups including Muslims, Dalits, and Christians (Banaji and Bhat 2019). The Hindu nationalist ideology promoted by prime minister Narendra Modi and his Bharatiya Janata Party (BJP) have amplified the denigration of minorities. Muslims in particular, as India's largest religious minority, are a major target for oppression and disinformation.

In parallel to these political developments, India experienced an explosive growth in digital media (Aneez et al. 2019) to become WhatsApp's largest market with some 230 million users (Kumar and Kumar 2018). Almost one in six of the country's WhatsApp groups are affiliated with political parties (ibid.). In addition to relatively standard 'get out the vote' political messaging, these groups promote disinformation about political actors and ferment Hindu–Muslim polarisation (Mahapatra and Plagemann 2019). False rumours implicating minorities in child kidnappings and cow slaughters have circulated rapidly on WhatsApp and have been linked to more than a hundred killings between 2015 and 2019 (Banaji and Bhat 2019).

In response to the Indian government's calls for intervention, WhatsApp undertook some measures to limit the size of groups and to make the mass forwarding of messages more difficult. However, these restrictions were circumvented by WhatsApp group owners – including the BJP – by increasing the number of groups they operate. At the same time, India's main political parties have adopted aggressive digital media strategies. In advance of the 2019 election, the BJP mobilised some 1.2 million volunteers to drive its digital campaign (Perrigo 2019), which was characterised by the use of data brokers to access voters' contact details and the dissemination of apps and games that were preloaded on free or low-cost phones (see Mahapatra and Plagemann 2019). Prime minister Narendra Modi has a dedicated app (NaMo) that has been linked to a network of disinformation outlets and the dissemination of polarising information (Bansal 2019).

At the international level, the proliferation of Indian disinformation is less deadly, but pervasive. In 2019, a report by the EU's East StratCom Task Force revealed that an Indian-run website (eptoday.com) was styling itself as a magazine for the European Parliament. It re-published a large amount of content from Russia Today while advancing Indian interests, particularly in relation to India's conflict with Pakistan (EUvsDisinfo 2019). A subsequent investigation by EU DisInfo Lab (2019) uncovered a global influence network managed by think tanks and NGOs clustered around the Srivastava Group, a New Delhi-based think tank. Although the network targeted elite decision makers and lobbied for Indian interests, no formal ties to the Indian government were identified (ibid.).

Principally, the network consisted of fake news websites with localised names including *The Times of Portugal* and *The Times of Geneva*. The latter appeared to target UN decision-makers with content critical of Pakistan's position in the Kashmir conflict. By quoting and referencing each other, this labyrinth of fake outlets were able to create the appearance of depth and credibility for their stories. Overall, EU DisInfo Lab (2019) identified 265 fake media outlets using a similar modus operandi in more than 65 countries. A similar operation was recently disclosed in Canadian Federal Court proceedings (Bell 2020). Court documents indicate that Canadian security officials suspected two branches of Indian intelligence – the Research and Analysis Wing and the Indian Intelligence Bureau – of attempting to influence Canadian politicians since 2009. The chief suspect accused of espionage was identified as the editor-in-chief of an unnamed Indian newspaper.

Meanwhile, the Indian government argues that it faces a national security threat from Chinese technology companies. In June 2020, the country banned 59 apps developed by Chinese firms including TikTok (Singh 2020). The Trump administration similarly argues that the popular TikTok app is a disinformation and security risk by enabling the Chinese Communist Party to harvest data about US citizens. In sum, the domestic and international dimensions of India's disinformation problem present a stark example of how bad actors can exploit social divisions to manipulate the information environment, but it is also indicative of how fears about disinformation and technology are weaponised in contemporary geo-politics.

Conclusion

It is relatively easy to create and distribute disinformation and, in general, there are few repercussions for doing so. In contrast, it is quite difficult to uncover and understand the operation of disinformation campaigns. In these circumstances, there is a natural tendency to focus on the tactics of bad actors and the content they create in isolation from wider contexts. However, individual disinformation campaigns are fundamentally entangled in social, political, cultural, and economic contexts and their campaigns – with varying levels of sophistication – transcend online and offline distinctions. Understanding these dynamics and developing a clearer picture of their impacts is a major challenge. By focusing on the volume of disinformation content, there is a real danger of overstating its impact (see Guess et al. 2020) and advocating hasty remedies. To this end, we suggest the overall threat of bad actors has less to do with individual pieces of disinformation than their sustained assault on evidence-based reasoning and trust in information. In other words, the true success of bad actors is the erosion of common ground for deliberation and communication. In the short term, countering bad actors requires finding ways to detect and limit their behaviours, but over the long term it requires finding ways to restore trust in the information environment (see Chapter 6).

References

Adaval R, Saluja G and Jiang Y (2018) Seeing and thinking in pictures: A review of visual information processing. *Consumer Psychology Review*. DOI: 10.1002/arcp.1049.

Applebaum A (2020) *Twilight of Democracy: The Seductive Lure of Authoritarianism*. First edition. New York: Doubleday.

Asenbaum H (2018) Anonymity and democracy: absence as presence in the public sphere. *American Political Science Review* 112(3): 459–472. DOI: 10.1017/S0003055418000163.

Avaaz (2019) *Far Right Networks of Deception*. London: Avaaz.

Bajomi-Lázár P (2019) An anti-migration campaign and its impact on public opinion: The Hungarian case. *European Journal of Communication* 34(6): 619–628. DOI: 10.1177/0267323119886152.

Bakir V and McStay A (2018) Fake news and the economy of emotions: problems, causes, solutions. *Digital Journalism* 6(2): 154–175. DOI: 10.1080/21670811.2017.1345645.

Banaji S and Bhat R (2019) *WhatsApp Vigilantes: An Exploration of Citizen Reception and Circulation of WhatsApp Misinformation Linked to Mob Violence in India*. London: London School of Economics. Available at: http://eprints.lse.ac.uk/104316/1/Banaji_whatsapp_vigilantes_exploration_of_citizen_reception_published.pdf.

Bansal S (2019) Narendra Modi App Has A Fake News Problem. *Huff Post*, 27 January. Available at: www.huffingtonpost.in/entry/narendra-modi-app-has-a-fake-news-problem_in_5c4d5c86e4b0287e5b8b6d52?guccounter=2.

Barrett B (2018) For Russia, unraveling US democracy was just another day job. *Wired*, 17 February. Available at: www.wired.com/story/mueller-indictment-internet-research-agency/.

Bell S (2020) Canadian politicians were targets of Indian intelligence covert influence operation: document. *Global News*, 17 April. Available at: https://globalnews.ca/news/6823170/canadian-politicians-targeted-indian-intelligence/.

Boykoff M and Farrell J (2019) Climate change countermovement organizations and media attention in the United States. In: Almiro N and Xifra J (eds) *Climate Change Denial and Public Relations: Strategic Communication and Interest Groups in Climate Inaction.* New York: Routledge, pp. 121–139.

Bradshaw S and Howard P (2019) *The Global Disinformation Order: 2019 Global Inventory of Organised Social Media Manipulation.* Oxford: Oxford Internet Institute.

Brennen S, Simon F, Howard P et al. (2020) *Types, Sources, and Claims of Covid-19 Misinformation.* 4 July. Oxford: Reuters Institute for the Study of Journalism. Available at: https://reutersinstitute.politics.ox.ac.uk/types-sources-and-claims-covid-19-misinformation.

Brüggemann M and Engesser S (2017) Beyond false balance: How interpretive journalism shapes media coverage of climate change. *Global Environmental Change* 42: 58–67. DOI: 10.1016/j.gloenvcha.2016.11.004.

Coleman S (2018) The elusiveness of political truth: From the conceit of objectivity to intersubjective judgement. *European Journal of Communication* 33(2): 157–171. DOI: 10.1177/0267323118760319.

Cook J (2019) Understanding and countering misinformation about climate change. In: Chiluwa I and Samoilenko S (eds) *Handbook of Research on Deception, Fake News, and Misinformation Online.* Hershey, PA: IGI-Globa, pp. 281–306.

Cook J, Lewandowsky S and Ecker UKH (2017) Neutralizing misinformation through inoculation: Exposing misleading argumentation techniques reduces their influence. Manalo E (ed.) *PLOS ONE* 12(5): e0175799. DOI: 10.1371/journal.pone.0175799.

Cook J, van der Linden SL, Lewandowsky S et al. (2020) Coronavirus, 'Plandemic' and the seven traits of conspiratorial thinking. *The Conversation*, 15 May. Available at: https://theconversation.com/coronavirus-plandemic-and-the-seven-traits-of-conspiratorial-thinking-138483.

Crandall CS, Miller JM and White MH (2018) Changing norms following the 2016 U.S. Presidential Election: The Trump effect on prejudice. *Social Psychological and Personality Science* 9(2): 186–192. DOI: 10.1177/1948550617750735.

Culloty E (2020) Conspiracy and the epistemological challenges of mediatised conflict. In: Maltby S, O'Loughlin B, Parry K et al. (eds) *Spaces of War, War of Spaces.* New York: Bloomsbury Academic.

Davey J and Ebner J (2017) *The Fringe Insurgency. Connectivity, Convergence and Mainstreaming of the Extreme Right.* London: Institute for Strategic Dialogue.

Ekman M (2019) Anti-immigration and racist discourse in social media. *European Journal of Communication* 34(6): 606–618. DOI: 10.1177/0267323119886151.

ERGA (2020) *ERGA Report on disinformation: Assessment of the implementation of the Code of Practice.* Brussels: European Regulators Group for Audiovisual Media Services (ERGA).

EU DisinfoLab (2019) *Influencing Policymakers with Fake Media Outlets: An Investigation into a Pro-Indian Influence Network.* Brussels: EU DisinfoLab.

EUvsDisinfo (2019) How to get the European Parliament to read Russia Today. *EUvsDisinfo*, 9 October. Available at: https://euvsdisinfo.eu/how-to-get-the-european-parliament-to-read-russia-today/.

Evans R (n.d.) How Coronavirus disinformation gets past social media moderators. In: *Bellingcat*. Available at: www.bellingcat.com/news/2020/04/03/how-coronavirus-disinformation-gets-past-social-media-moderators/.

Freelon D and Lokot T (2020) Russian disinformation campaigns on Twitter target political communities across the spectrum. Collaboration between opposed political groups might be the most effective way to counter it. *Harvard Kennedy School Misinformation Review.* DOI: 10.37016/mr-2020-003.

Froio C and Ganesh B (2019) The transnationalisation of far right discourse on Twitter: Issues and actors that cross borders in Western European democracies. *European Societies* 21(4): 513–539. DOI: 10.1080/14616696.2018.1494295.

Fung B and Garcia A (2019) Facebook has shut down 5.4 billion fake accounts this year. *CNN*, 13 November. Available at: https://edition.cnn.com/2019/11/13/tech/facebook-fake-accounts/index.html.

Ganesh B (2018) The ungovernability of digital hate culture. *Journal of International Affairs* 71(2): 30–49.

Ging D (2019) Alphas, betas, and incels: Theorizing the masculinities of the manosphere. *Men and Masculinities* 22(4): 638–657. DOI: 10.1177/1097184X17706401.

Global Disinformation Index (2019) *The Quarter Billion Dollar Question: How is Disinformation Gaming Ad Tech?* 4 September. London: Global Disinformation Index.

Gorwa R and Guilbeault D (2020) Unpacking the social media bot: A typology to guide research and policy. *Policy & Internet* 12(2): 225–248. DOI: 10.1002/poi3.184.

Graham R (2016) Inter-ideological mingling: White extremist ideology entering the mainstream on Twitter. *Sociological Spectrum* 36(1): 24–36. DOI: 10.1080/02732173.2015.1075927.

Guess AM, Nyhan B and Reifler J (2020) Exposure to untrustworthy websites in the 2016 US election. *Nature Human Behaviour* 4(5): 472–480. DOI: 10.1038/s41562-020-0833-x.

Habermas J (1984) *The Theory of Communicative Action.* Boston: Beacon Press.

Harambam J (2020) *Contemporary Conspiracy Culture: Truth and Knowledge in an Era of Epistemic Instability. Conspiracy Theories* . Abingdon: Routledge.

Hartzell SL (n.d.) Alt-White: Conceptualizing the 'Alt-Right' as a rhetorical bridge between White nationalism and mainstream public discourse. *Journal of Contemporary Rhetoric* 8(1/2): 6–25.

Hope M (2019) Revealed: How the tobacco and fossil fuel industries fund disinformation campaigns around the world. In: *Desmog UK.* Available at: www.desmog.co.uk/2019/02/19/how-tobacco-and-fossil-fuel-companies-fund-disinformation-campaigns-around-world.

Hope Not Hate (2019) *State of Hate 2019: People Vs the Elite*. London: Hope Not Hate.

Iasiello E (2016) China's three warfares strategy mitigates fallout from cyber espionage activities. *Journal of Strategic Security* 9(2): 47–71. DOI: 10.5038/1944-0472.9.2.1489.

Institute for Strategic Dialogue (2019) ISD research featured in POLITICO about the trolling of the UN migration pact. In: *Institute for Strategic Dialogue*. Available at: www.isdglobal.org/isd-research-featured-in-politico-surroundingthe-trolling-of-the-un-migration-pact/.

Karpf D (2019) On digital disinformation and democratic myths. *Media Well*, 10 December. Available at: https://mediawell.ssrc.org/expert-reflections/on-digital-disinformation-and-democratic-myths/.

Kumar S and Kumar P (2018) How widespread is WhatsApp's usage in India? *Live Mint*, 18 July. Available at: www.livemint.com/Technology/O6DLmIibCCV5luEG9XuJWL/How-widespread-is-WhatsApps-usage-in-India.html.

Lanoszka A (2019) Disinformation in international politics. *European Journal of International Security* 4(2): 227–248. DOI: 10.1017/eis.2019.6.

Lou C and Yuan S (2019) Influencer marketing: How message value and credibility affect consumer trust of branded content on social media. *Journal of Interactive Advertising* 19(1): 58–73. DOI: 10.1080/15252019.2018.1533501.

Mahapatra S and Plagemann J (2019) *Polarisation and Politicisation: The Social Media Strategies of Indian Political Parties*. Hamburg: German Institute of Global and Area Studies. Available at: https://nbn-resolving.org/urn:nbn:de:0168-ssoar-61811–8.

Marwick A and Lewis R (2017) *Media Manipulation and Disinformation Online*. New York: Data & Society.

Molina MD, Sundar SS, Le T et al. (2019) 'Fake news' is not simply false information: A concept explication and taxonomy of online content. *American Behavioral Scientist*. DOI: 10.1177/0002764219878224.

Murphy K (2020) Google detecting 18m malware and phishing messages per day related to Covid-19. *The Guardian*, 13 July. Available at: www.theguardian.com/australia-news/2020/jul/14/google-detecting-18m-malware-and-phishing-messages-per-day-related-to-covid-19.

Nimmo B, François C, Eib CS et al. (2020) *Exposing Secondary Infektion*. New York: Graphika. Available at: https://graphika.com/reports/exposing-secondary-infektion/.

Ong JC and Cabañes JV (2018) *Architects of Networked Disinformation*. Leeds: University of Leeds.

Papenfuss M (2019) Facebook shuts down Pro-Trump page run by Ukrainians. *Huff Post*, 23 September. Available at: www.huffpost.com/entry/facebook-i-love-america-pro-trump-page_n_5d8945b6e4b0938b5932da48?guccounter=1&guce_referrer=aHR0cHM6Ly9kdWNrZHVja2dvLmNvbNvbS8&guce_referrer_sig=AQAAAE1ANeTM0i-25eTQyTsDtzdNGb-7BCgdzyH3N9y3dYcmY1dQyNktfLrwDfJImTDaalhHTgD4zL3bWreqKoH0y8Etp9iB6qtjrH1nqSjdndgwvZvqMaMNFxCS0fB1cO15HKbtsuABFfQQa4wNfj4RbgxuY7pXWakpWMyX6VOQ_tj6.

Paris B and Donovan J (2019) *Deepfakes and Cheap Fakes The Manipulation of Audio and Visual Evidence*. New York: Data & Society. Available at: https://datasociety.net/library/deepfakes-and-cheap-fakes/.

Paschen J (2019) Investigating the emotional appeal of fake news using artificial intelligence and human contributions. *Journal of Product & Brand Management* 29(2): 223–233. DOI: 10.1108/JPBM-12-2018-2179.

Perrigo B (2019) How volunteers for India's ruling party are using WhatsApp to fuel fake news ahead of elections. *Time*, 25 January. Available at: https://time.com/5512032/whatsapp-india-election-2019/.

Plaugic L (2016) Google pulls Chrome extension that marked Jewish people online. *The Verge*, 3 June. Available at: www.theverge.com/2016/6/3/11853244/google-chrome-extension-jewish-people-pulled.

Rawnsley A (2020) Conservative sites like Newsmax and Washington Examiner have published Middle East hot takes from 'experts' who are actually fake personas pushing propaganda. *The Daily Beast*, 7 July. Available at: www.thedailybeast.com/right-wing-media-outlets-duped-by-a-middle-east-propaganda-campaign.

Readfearn G (2016) Revealed: Most popular climate story on social media told half a million people the science was a hoax. In: *Desmog*. Available at: www.desmogblog.com/2016/11/29/revealed-most-popular-climate-story-social-media-told-half-million-people-science-was-hoax.

Rosenberg E (2011) CNN, MSNBC ran more birther coverage than Fox News. *The Atlantic*, 28 April. Available at: www.theatlantic.com/politics/archive/2011/04/chart-cnn-msnbc-ran-more-birther-coverage-fox-news/350112/.

Sandbothe M (1998) Media temporalities in the internet: Philosophy of time and media with Derrida and Rorty. *Journal of Computer-Mediated Communication* 4(2): 0–0. DOI: 10.1111/j.1083–6101.1998.tb00091.x.

Seib PM (2016) *The Future of Diplomacy*. Cambridge, UK; Malden, MA: Polity Press.

Shao C, Ciampaglia GL, Varol O et al. (2018) The spread of low-credibility content by social bots. *Nature Communications* 9(1): 4787. DOI: 10.1038/s41467-018-06930-7.

Siapera E, Boudourides M, Lenis S et al. (2018) Refugees and network publics on twitter: Networked framing, affect, and capture. *Social Media + Society* 4(1). DOI: 10.1177/2056305118764437.

Singh M (2020) India bans TikTok, dozens of other Chinese apps. *Tech Crunch*, 29 June.

Tomkinson S, Harper T and Attwell K (2020) Confronting Incel: Exploring possible policy responses to misogynistic violent extremism. *Australian Journal of Political Science* 55(2): 152–169. DOI: 10.1080/10361146.2020.1747393.

Vargo CJ, Guo L and Amazeen MA (2018) The agenda-setting power of fake news: A big data analysis of the online media landscape from 2014 to 2016. *New Media & Society* 20(5): 2028–2049. DOI: 10.1177/1461444817712086.

Wardle C and Derakhshan H (2017) *Information Disorder: Toward an Interdisciplinary Framework for Research and Policy Making*. DGI(2017)09. Brussels: Council of Europe.

Warzel C (2017) Alex Jones Just Can't Help Himself. *Buzzfeed*, 3 May. Available at: www.buzzfeednews.com/article/charliewarzel/alex-jones-will-never-stop-being-alex-jones.

Wells C, Shah DV, Pevehouse JC et al. (2016) How Trump drove coverage to the nomination: Hybrid media campaigning. *Political Communication* 33(4): 669–676. DOI: 10.1080/10584609.2016.1224416.

Yablokov I (2015) Conspiracy theories as a Russian public diplomacy tool: The case of Russia Today (RT). *Politics* 35(3–4): 301–315. DOI: 10.1111/1467-9256.12097.

Young VA (2020) Nearly half of the Twitter accounts discussing 'reopening America' may be bots. In: *Carnegie Mellon University*. Available at: www.cmu.edu/news/stories/archives/2020/may/twitter-bot-campaign.html.

Zuckerman E (2019) QAnon and the emergence of the unreal. *Journal of Design and Science* (6). DOI: 10.21428/7808da6b.6b8a82b9.

3 Platforms

In the Global North, the advent of the internet was widely welcomed as a democratising force that greatly expanded access to information and freedom of expression. Led by the US, democratic states championed a global internet and advocated lax regulation to allow online companies to flourish. Internet governance was largely conceived in terms of managing technical standards and domain names while online companies were treated as neutral platforms and exempt from liability for the content they hosted. In the early 1990s, few could have anticipated how online technologies would evolve, but the expectation that public goods and democratic values would follow from digital innovation proved to be a delusion 'with significant global consequences that may risk undermining the very project of promoting democracy' (Morozov 2011: xvii).

Far from the vision of a 'free and open internet' (Clinton 2011), the online world is dominated by a small group of companies including Amazon, Google, and Facebook. While these platforms began with a niche focus – online shopping, web search, social networking – they have grown into vast infrastructures upon which entire sectors of social and economic life are dependent (Plantin and Punathambekar 2019). Part of their power lies in their 'intermediation bias' whereby platform algorithms influence the content people see and are likely to engage with (Calvano and Polo 2020). Consequently, as traditional industries moved online, their business models were subsumed by the platforms' model of 'surveillance capitalism' (Zuboff 2019). Within this model, internet users are offered free access to content while platforms accumulate users' personal data, often without their knowledge, and generate revenue through personalised advertising and other data-based services. In this way, the major platforms – Google and Facebook in particular – dominate the online advertising market by allowing advertisers to target audiences across a range of personalised dimensions including demographics, personal interests, browsing history, and so on.

Antitrust and consumer protection authorities have struggled to keep pace with these developments (Wu 2017). The platforms have been given free rein to buy-up competitors and new entrants to the market. Google has acquired more than 230 companies including YouTube while Facebook has acquired more than 80 companies including Instagram (Lemoine 2020). Now, amid the 'backlash against Big Tech' (Ovide 2020), regulators are rolling back on their lax oversight. A report by the UK's Digital, Media, Culture, and Sport Committee (2019: 42) described platforms as 'digital gangsters' that consider 'themselves to be ahead of and beyond the law'. In July 2020, the chairman of the US House of Representatives' Antitrust Subcommittee deemed Facebook's acquisition of Instagram to be illegal and questioned whether Instagram should be broken off into a separate company (Hatmaker 2020). Whether or not antitrust actions materialise remains to be seen. In any case, additional action is required to implement mechanisms that would allow third parties to hold platforms accountable on behalf of users. Viewed from the lens of surveillance capitalism, disinformation and related information pathologies cannot be isolated from the platforms' wider system of data harvesting, targeted advertising, and 'attention brokerage' (Wu 2017).

The opaqueness surrounding the use of personal data was a key consideration behind the development of the EU's General Data Protection Regulation (GDPR), which has heightened awareness of data harvesting and digital ethics more generally. Regarding disinformation specifically, there are major questions about how to regulate the political use of bots, microtargeted advertising, and 'deepfake' technologies (see Chapter 5). As such, debates about regulations on data protection are 'no longer serving only the protection of private individuals, but also safeguarding public values, including democracy' (Brkan 2019: 71). To examine these issues, this chapter first outlines two major features of the platform's business models – algorithms and advertising – and assesses the impact on the information environment including the destabilisation of quality journalism. We then consider governance proposals that aim to enhance transparency and accountability. Finally, in the case study, we highlight how YouTube's search and recommendation facilities subvert information seekers to promote conspiracy theorists and extremist ideologies.

Algorithms

The development of effective algorithms to locate and filter web content is an important development in the history of the web. While early search engines relied on directories of websites that were categorised by humans or web crawlers, by the mid-1990s these approaches were totally insufficient to accommodate the rapid growth of the web. Sophisticated algorithms, such as the PageRank algorithm underpinning Google Search, 'brought order to chaos by offering a clean and seamless interface to deliver content to users' (Hoffman et al. 2019: 10). In principle, algorithms offer enormous opportunities for positive social impact (Shah 2018), but, in the current environment, they afford a handful of companies the power to manage how information is received and perceived (Langlois and Elmer 2013). The platforms that capitalised on these capabilities introduced a new model of content consumption whereby feeds of content are determined by algorithms and optimised for user engagement and advertising. For example, the default setting for Facebook's NewsFeed, is not, as one might expect, a chronological presentation of posts by the friends, groups, and pages a user has chosen to engage with. Rather, it is algorithmically generated based on predictions about relevance and engagement (Hoffmann et al. 2019).

As platform algorithms play a central role in influencing what people see online, an entire marketing industry has been built around understanding how algorithms rank and prioritise information. As Gillespie (2017: 64) explains, 'every contribution to the public web in some way desires to be seen, which generally requires being recognised and amplified by Google'. Strategists within the search engine optimisation (SEO) and social media marketing industries monitor algorithms to find ways to increase the visibility of their clients' content (see Hoffman et al. 2019). These are the same strategies that enable disinformation actors to manipulate algorithms. For example, an investigation by *The Guardian* found that Google Search and its autocomplete function have been manipulated to prioritise websites that declare climate change is a hoax, being gay is a sin, and the Sandy Hook mass shooting never happened (Solon and Levin 2016). In other instances, bad actors exploit knowledge gaps or 'data voids' in search engines. For example, Golebiewski and boyd (2018) describe how white nationalists promote uncommon search terms, such as 'black on white crimes', that return extremist content in the search results.

Platform algorithms are dynamic and major changes can have dramatic knock-on effects across entire sectors. Most controversially, Facebook encouraged publishers and advertisers to 'pivot to video' production based on flawed metrics about users' engagement with video content. In response, some media outlets replaced writers with video producers before pivoting back to text when it became clear that the level of video engagement was overstated (Madrigal and Meyer 2018). In 2019, Facebook agreed a settlement with advertisers who alleged the company inflated video engagement metrics by 150 to 900 per cent (AP 2019). In response to criticism about their role in disseminating disinformation, Facebook and Google both introduced major algorithmic changes. However, as Tromble and McGregor (2019) argue, social media companies continue to view disinformation as a design problem that can be addressed with algorithmic tweaks and changes in the user interface.

Although the platforms typically claim that their algorithms are neutral tools or a means to serve users' needs with personalised experiences, it is difficult to verify those claims. The algorithms that dominate our online lives are mostly proprietary and so inaccessible to independent scrutiny. On this basis, Pasquale argues (2015) that we live in a 'black box society' in which human expertise has been replaced by algorithmic decision-making. Unsurprisingly, the ubiquity of algorithms and their power in our daily lives has led to increasing calls for algorithmic transparency and accountability (Ananny and Crawford 2018; Veale, et al. 2018). Reduced to their technical description, algorithms are merely sets of instructions that computers employ to carry out a task. However, 'there is also no such thing as a raw algorithm in terms of it being seen as an uncomplicated and objective instruction' (Wilson 2017: 141). Instead, 'algorithms are embedded in complex amalgams of political, technical, cultural, and social interactions' (ibid.). There are now many examples of algorithmic bias including racial and gender biases that are built into algorithms through the use of unrepresentative training data and the biases of those involved in the design process (Garfinkel et al. 2017; Turner Lee et al. 2019). Clearly, there is a need for close scrutiny of how algorithms are designed, by whom, and for what purpose. In this regard, Ananny and Crawford (2018) argue that accountability is quite different from mere transparency. Put simply, if transparency means peering into the 'black box' of algorithmic models, it may do little to illuminate their impact or to improve the environment. After all, even the engineers who develop machine-learning algorithms may not fully understand how they operate (Gillespie 2018).

Moreover, algorithms are only one node in the broader system. In the case of Google and Facebook, algorithms serve the backbone of their business: advertising. By prioritising user engagement, powerful algorithms consolidated the rise of 'surveillance capitalism': the capacity to generate economic value from the accumulation of personal data (Zuboff 2019). By tracking online behaviour, using technologies such as 'cookies', platforms gather data about users' habits, practices, and attitudes. With this data, they develop even more sophisticated algorithms for analysing and predicting online behaviour. It is this accumulation of personalised data that opened up new ground for online advertising and digital marketing, as outlined below.

Advertising

Platforms operate as multi-sided businesses: their consumer-facing products compete for audience attention and this attention, and the personal data surrounding it, is then resold to advertisers on the other side of the market (Wu 2017). Of course, platforms did not invent this business model. In the mass media age, most news outlets offered consumers a cheap service and only met the costs of production – and earned a profit – by matching advertisers to their consumer base. The major platforms offer their services for free, but, given their enormous reach, the advertising capabilities and revenues far exceed that of traditional media. In particular, what separates the platforms from their mass media predecessors is the ability to target advertising at the individual level. In their analysis of internet economics, Calvano and Polo (2020) note that seven of the ten most popular websites in the US are in the business of harvesting attention that can be resold to advertisers. Arguing from an antitrust perspective, Wu (2017) observes a legal failure to recognise that these companies all operate in the same market. Regardless of whether they are search engines or social networks, they generate revenue by acting as 'attention brokers' that accumulate data for advertising (ibid.).

Microtargeting is a marketing strategy that collects user data – demographic, psychographic, geographic, behavioural – to segment people into distinct groups for advertising. It is an extension of the socio-economic classifications used in traditional advertising. Google supports targeting based on demographics, interests, online behaviour patterns, and similarities to other audience groups while Facebook offers additional categories including income level and 'ethnic affinity' (see Kreiss and McGregor 2019). As Ryan (2019) argues, there is little regulation over the use of this personal data and it forms the basis of the programmatic advertising described below. In the US, the Department of Housing and Urban Development sued Facebook for violating the Fair Housing Act by allowing advertisers to discriminate against users based on race, gender, and other characteristics (Tobin 2019). Microtargeting is perhaps most controversial in relation to political advertising as the dominance of US platforms has led to a largely unquestioned adherence to the US model of permitting political advertising as a form of free expression (Marsden et al. 2020). Consequently, many countries have an imbalanced approach whereby offline political advertising is highly regulated, but online political advertising is not. Importantly, it is the lack of transparency surrounding online political advertising and the role of private companies in regulating it that make the practice undemocratic. These issues are distinct from claims about the influence of microtargeting on voter behaviour. Irrespective of any influence on politics, Facebook and Google have a duty to explain and defend their decisions to their users and the public at large (Kreiss and McGregor 2019).

With microtargeting, bad actors can target those whose personality and behavioural characteristics make them more likely to consume, believe, and spread disinformation (Kosinski et al. 2013). However, it is important to avoid overstating the power of these practices. To a large extent, claims about the capabilities of microtargeting and user profiling are part of the platforms' own business hype and so we should be 'cautious to impute to Facebook magical powers of persuasion' (Benkler et al. 2018: 279). These nuances are exemplified by the Cambridge Analytica scandal. Cambridge Analytica marketed itself as a political consulting company that combined data-analytics and psychographic profiling to tailor 'messages that had been carefully crafted precisely for' voters' unique characteristics, beliefs, and vulnerabilities (Kaiser 2019: 25). The company fraudulently harvested Facebook data from millions of users and employed psychologists to design Facebook quizzes that would capture respondents' personality traits and political attitudes. However, there is little evidence to support the claim that tailored adverts can influence voting behaviour (see Benkler et al. 2018). As Benkler et al. (2018: 279) argue, 'using tailored advertisements to change hearts and minds, and more importantly voter behaviour, is still primarily an act of faith, much like most of the rest of online advertising'. Despite the hype surrounding digital marketing, there is a surprising lack of evidence to support its effectiveness.

Researchers at Facebook and Northwestern University tested the causal effects of digital advertising using randomised controlled trials and then compared the results to the observational metrics used within the industry (Gordon et al. 2017). While industry metrics greatly overstated the effectiveness of advertising, the experimental studies indicated that outcomes were due to selection effects rather than advertising effects. In other words, most of the people who purchased a service after viewing adverts would have purchased without seeing the adverts. It remains debatable whether the vast amounts of money spent on digital advertising are good value for the companies who purchase them. What is clear, however, is that the shifts in the advertising market have had a detrimental effect on quality news media while also creating revenue streams for bad actors.

News media have struggled to adjust to the digital environment where they have encountered increased competition from new media sources, changing patterns of audience consumption, and a dramatic decline in revenue (Anderson et al. 2015; Elvestad and Phillips 2018). Historically, news media relied heavily on advertising revenue, but advertisers now have access to a wider range of online sources (Anderson et al. 2015) and online advertising is dominated by Google and Facebook who control 51 per cent of the global market (Graham 2019). In these conditions, the economic viability of the news media sector is severely undermined; local and regional news outlets are closing and major outlets have imposed significant staff layoffs. These conditions have major implications for the type of costly investigative reporting that serves the public interest and it opens up the news media sector to capture by financial interests and a further concentration of media ownership (Nielsen 2017; Stiglitz 2017).

Ryan (2019) argues that programmatic advertising and real-time bidding (RTB) are particularly destructive for quality news media because it has transformed the practice of 'media buying' into 'target-audience buying'. This is possible because massive amounts of 'cookie' data are used to track users' online behaviour. When a user visits a website, an ad-exchange automatically evaluates advertising bids based on the user's profile and then serves the advert from the winner bidder to the user on the website. The benefits for advertisers are clear. As *Digiday*, an online trade magazine, enthuses, 'thanks to real-time bidding, ad buyers no longer need to work directly with publishers or ad networks to negotiate ad prices and to traffic ads' (Marshall 2014). However, user profiling undercuts quality publishers because it allows advertisers to target the consumers of quality brands without paying for advertising on the websites of those brands. That is, advertisers can target the consumers who have visited a publishers' website while placing their adverts on a 'less reputable website at an enormous discount' (Ryan 2019).

As noted in Chapter 2, the ad-tech industry generates revenue for bad actors by driving traffic to websites that sell advertising. The value of advertising on disinformation websites is estimated at €200 million annually (Global Disinformation Index 2019). The essence of the problem is that the platforms do not screen the websites for which they provide advertising services. Consequently, the platforms and major brands inadvertently fund disinformation. The Global Disinformation Index (2020) estimates that Google provides $3 out of every $4 in ad revenue earned by disinformation sites. In addition, major brands unwittingly fund disinformation as their adverts are placed on disinformation sites. For example, during the Covid-19 crisis, adverts from major healthcare brands, including Merck and Johnson & Johnson, were placed on disinformation sites promoting Covid-19 conspiracy theories (ibid.). Quite apart from the social harms that arise from funding disinformation, these practices are clearly damaging to the reputation of brands. During Covid-19 and the Black Lives Matter protests, Facebook became a target of brand action; although the temporary suspension of advertising was somewhat superficial (Tassi 2020). More sustained and coordinated brand action may have some impact on platform practices over time, but the crux of the issue is a matter of governance.

Governance

Bowers and Zittrain (2019) describe three eras of internet governance: the rights era, the public health era, and the process era. Beginning in the 1990s, the rights era is synonymous with John Perry Barlow's (1996) 'Declaration of the Independence of Cyberspace'. Arguing from a libertarian perspective, Barlow characterised the internet as a new territory for freedom of expression that should be free from government regulations. Over the past decade, this argument has been contested by those highlighting the public harms that arise from unregulated speech including the proliferation of illegal content (e.g. terrorist and child abuse content) as well as harmful content such as disinformation. Bowers and Zittrain (2019) suggest that these debates are now giving way to a process era focused on the development of mechanisms that can balance rights and public health interests.

For their part, the platforms have responded by appointing chief ethics officers to oversee the application of artificial intelligence technologies and the potential misuse of data (Bean 2020). Regarding content specifically, Facebook revealed the 20 members of its Oversight Board in May 2020 (Clegg 2020). Previously, Mark Zuckerberg (quoted in Klein 2018) described the intention to create a 'Supreme Court' type structure composed of independent adjudicators 'who ultimately make the final judgment call on what should be acceptable speech in a community that reflects the social norms and values of people all around the world'. It is clearly fanciful to assume that 20 individuals – a quarter of whom are from the US and the majority of whom are legal experts – can reflect the interests of Facebook users across the world. Moreover, the Board's remit is restricted to evaluating content removal decisions rather than issues relating to the company's algorithmic and advertising practices (see Ingram 2020). As currently formulated, the Board is unlikely to have any impact on the proliferation of disinformation and related problem content.

The key issue for governance is whether platforms can implement appropriate mechanisms within their own structures or whether regulators will develop mechanisms that operate independent of the platforms (Bowers and Zittrain 2019). Given the pervasiveness of platforms' reach into social and economic life, the need for standards concerns a wide range of areas including data protection, content moderation, algorithmic accountability, competition policy, and electoral integrity. Addressing these areas requires multiple and overlapping forms of governance that engage the platforms, civil society, and states. The development of governance structures is complicated by the fact that platforms are international businesses and state-based governance mechanisms have historically struggled to address the influence of transnational corporations (Gowra 2019). In this context, Gowra (2019: 15) suggests that self-regulatory codes and multi-stakeholder regulatory standards 'often are the best out of a slew of bad options'. Similarly, Marsden et al. (2020) argue that it is not desirable to give states the power to regulate disinformation just as it is not desirable to allow platforms to regulate themselves. In contrast, a co-regulatory model allows platforms to develop mechanisms to regulate their own users whereby these mechanisms are approved and monitored by state regulators.

As outlined in Chapter 5, the European Union is taking steps in this direction. In 2018, the EU implemented the Code of Practice on Disinformation (European Commission 2018), which was signed by the major platforms as well as digital advertising bodies. Under this self-regulatory code, the platforms committed to develop safeguards against disinformation by increasing transparency around advertising and developing effective content policies (European Commission 2018). However, the EU's own evaluation of the Code's implementation identified serious shortcomings including the inability to sanction platforms for non-compliance (ERGA 2020). Regarding advertising practices, a separate EU report concluded that the code 'does not have a high enough public profile to put sufficient pressure for change on platforms' (European Commission 2020: 4). It is expected that the EU's Digital Services Act, due in 2021, will move away from a self-regulatory approach towards co-regulation and introduce liability for the content platforms' host.

Beyond the EU, there is no shortage of proposals for how to enhance accountability and transparency in platform governance.

Many of these are well considered. For example, the Santa Clara Principles (2018) were proposed by a group of academics and NGOs to introduce minimum levels of transparency and accountability for users whose content or accounts have been flagged or removed. In May 2019, New Zealand Prime Minister Jacinda Ardern and French President Emmanuel Macron unveiled the Christchurch Call, a non-binding set of commitments to combat terrorist content online that was signed by 18 governments and eight major technology firms. At the same time, human-rights advocates have raised concerns about the loss of valuable human-rights records as overzealous moderation results in the erroneous classification of 'extremist' content (Banchik 2020). In this context, the United Nations' Special Rapporteur on Freedom of Expression calls for a human rights approach to content moderation (Kaye 2018). Currently, the NGO Article 19 proposes the development of multi-stakeholder 'social media councils' that could advise on standards for content moderation and offer users a means to appeal platforms' decisions (Article 19 2019).

More broadly, there is the growing recognition that funding journalism is a priority for countering disinformation. News media publishers have long sought compensation from the platforms that distribute their content. Publishers in Germany, France, and Spain lobbied for national copyright laws that forced Google to pay for the snippets of news articles it features. Google's response was to stop showing news snippets in those countries (Wolde and Auchard 2014). The action also backfired by greatly reducing referral traffic to the publishers leading Axel Springer, Germany's largest news publisher, to reverse its stance on Google snippets (ibid.). Nevertheless, in 2020 the Australian government announced plans to force Google and Facebook to participate in a negotiating process with Australian news publishers. The plan will introduce minimum standards for the platforms' engagement with news media including advance notice of any algorithmic changes that will affect referral traffic or any design changes that will affect the presentation of news or the advertising associated with news (Nicholls 2020). To counteract disinformation, similar proposals could compel platforms to redistribute revenue to fact-checking and media and literacy initiatives (Marsden et al. 2020). Developing oversight mechanisms for the platforms is currently an area of much experimentation. However, as we argue in Chapter 5, much more research is required to understand the effectiveness of proposed countermeasures and the potential risks they pose to fundamental rights and the goals of advancing media pluralism and democracy.

Case study: disinformation on YouTube

Launched in 2005 and acquired by Google in 2006, YouTube plays a dominant role in digital communication and culture. Globally, it is the second most-visited website after Google.com (Alexa 2020). The popularity of YouTube typifies a broader shift towards online video consumption; a shift enabled by improvements in broadband internet speeds and the growth of mobile devices. Around 500 hours of video are uploaded to YouTube every minute and more than two billion account holders log in each month (YouTube 2020). With this large user base and opportunities to monetise content, YouTube is an attractive platform for both commercial media and amateur producers (see Burgess and Green 2018). However, YouTube's algorithm and business model are implicated in the promotion of conspiracy theories and extremist ideologies.

In 2019, the US Federal Bureau of Investigation described conspiracy theories as a domestic terrorism threat (Faddoul et al. 2020). There is anecdotal evidence that YouTube's recommendation algorithm directs people towards conspiracy theories (Tufekci 2018). Research studies also find that YouTube recommendations surface problem content including conspiracy theories (Alfano et al. 2020) and sexually suggestive content (Kaiser and Rauchfleisch 2019). A study in March 2020 found that one-quarter of the most viewed YouTube videos about Covid-19 contained misleading information (Li et al. 2020). The extent to which YouTube facilitates radicalisation is a major concern. Ribeiro et al. (2019) analysed comment sections to correlate users' pathways across videos over time and found that users consistently migrate from milder to more extreme content. In contrast, Ledwich and Zaitsev (2019) argue that YouTube is more likely to steer people away from extremist content because the algorithm privileges popularity and, in general, extremist content is not popular.

It is important to note that research in this area encounters several limitations. As YouTube constantly updates its algorithms, it is difficult to compare the results of different studies. Moreover, in the absence of cooperation from YouTube, it is difficult for researchers to develop a complete representation of the platform or to fully reflect the practices of actual users and the recommendations they receive. Few studies attempt to replicate the conditions of actual viewers with histories of previously watched videos. An exception is Hussein et al. (2020) who created more than 150 Google accounts and developed 'watch histories' to assess search results and recommendations for five conspiracy theory topics. They found that watch histories created a filter bubble effect by presenting less diverse and more attitude confirming search results and recommendations.

YouTube offers recommendations in several ways. Videos are suggested on the home-page, in personalised playlists, and in the 'up next' feature when auto-play is enabled. As with other proprietary algorithms, the operation of YouTube's recommendation system is not transparent to users or regulators. Nevertheless, Google researchers have explained how the 'most sophisticated industrial recommendation systems in existence' (Covington et al. 2016: 1) uses deep-learning neural networks to recommend videos based on a user's viewing history, the popularity of videos, and an effort to balance new content with well-established videos. Zhao et al. (2019) explain that video recommendations rely on multiple algorithms: one algorithm generates possible videos by matching the topic of the search query while another algorithm selects videos based on how often the video has been watched. The system then learns by evaluating user feedback in terms of engagement behaviour (e.g. clicks) and satisfaction behaviours (e.g. likes).

Of course, the ultimate metric for assessing the effectiveness of recommendations is 'watch time' rather than the quality of the videos (Covington et al. 2016). Although YouTube maintains that other, unstated, metrics shape the recommendation algorithm, it 'is unarguable, nevertheless, that keeping users engaged remains the main driver for YouTube's advertising revenues' (Faddoul et al. 2020: 1). In fact, YouTube claims that more than 70 per cent of users' viewing time is the result of algorithmic recommendation rather than purposeful choices (Solsman 2018). The premise of recommending videos without attending to quality is relatively benign for many types of content such as cat videos and music, but championing engagement over quality is clearly problematic when users are seeking out factual information. Moreover, as conspiracy theories and extremist content are often highly engaging, recommendation algorithms are potentially vulnerable to a feedback loop that reinforces disinformation (Faddoul et al. 2020).

In response to mounting criticisms, YouTube announced changes that aimed to demote and demonetise the most egregious conspiracy videos (Wong and Levin 2019). Based on a US experiment, YouTube reported that limiting 'recommendations of borderline content and harmful misinformation' had reduced watch time – arising from recommendations – by 50 per cent (YouTube 2019). In their longitudinal analysis of conspiracy theory videos, Faddoul et al. (2020) confirmed that YouTube did significantly reduce the overall volume of conspiratorial content in recommendations. However, they note that the volume of conspiratorial content remains relatively high and that aggregate data may obscure the filter-bubble effects described by Hussein et al. (2020). In other words, once users have engaged with conspiratorial and extremist content, they are likely to be presented with similar – and potentially more extreme – content.

As with other areas of disinformation, the lack of transparency and accountability greatly impedes the ability of researchers and regulators to assess the nature of disinformation on YouTube and the extent to which it contributes to radicalisation. Given YouTube's enormous computational resources, the company is clearly capable of detecting and mitigating disinformation (Faddoul et al. 2020). The question, however, is what level of oversight needs to be embedded in the corporate response.

Conclusion

The pace of technological change over the past 30 years has profoundly altered how information is produced and consumed, but legal and regulatory structures have not kept pace with these changes. The rules that exempt platforms from liability for the content they host were designed to encourage digital innovation, but have resulted in monopolies and the proliferation of illegal and harmful content. Similarly, regulatory structures for media were designed for a pre-internet world in which there were relatively clear boundaries between media production, distribution, and consumption. Irrespective of current concerns about disinformation, there has been an urgent need to update governance structures for many years. Importantly, the core issues of governance extend far beyond disinformation. Apart from monetising public attention, platforms have an unaccountable power to implement algorithmic and design changes that impact entire sectors and pay no heed to the public good. Moreover, if the early vision of a 'free and open internet' (Clinton 2011) is to be retained in any meaningful way, it must be upheld for countries beyond the Global North where the platforms are developing new markets in ways that are antithetical to internet freedom (Prasad 2018).

Regarding disinformation specifically, the technological affordances that underpin digital advertising enable the spread of disinformation while also undermining quality information. As such, it is difficult to see how specific actions to counter disinformation can succeed without attending to the deeper problems inherent to the platforms' business models. Fundamentally, platforms were never designed to function as a public sphere. Semantic debates about the distinction between platforms and publishers do little to address this issue (see Flew et al. 2019). Facebook and Google are not neutral platforms in the sense of a telecoms provider, but they are also not publishers in the traditional sense of a media outlet. They do far more than publish content and have a reach that is unthinkable for any traditional media outlet. As Farkas and Schou (2018) argue, concerns about disinformation have drawn attention to the infrastructural power of the platforms and their influence on public debate. Finding ways to address this power requires rethinking how platforms and emerging tech companies operate while also thinking about new ways to reinvigorate democratic participation.

References

Alexa (2020) Top Sites. In: *Alexa*. Available at: www.alexa.com/topsites.

Alfano M, Fard AE, Carter JA et al. (2020) Technologically scaffolded atypical cognition: The case of YouTube's recommender system. *Synthese*. DOI: 10.1007/s11229-020-02724-x.

Ananny M and Crawford K (2018) Seeing without knowing: Limitations of the transparency ideal and its application to algorithmic accountability. *New Media & Society* 20(3): 973–989. DOI: 10.1177/1461444816676645.

Anderson CW, Bell E and Shirky C (2015) Post-industrial journalism: Adapting to the present. *Geopolitics, History & International Relations* 7(2): 32–123.

AP (2019) Facebook to settle advertiser lawsuit for $40 million. *AP*, 8 October. Available at: https://apnews.com/41dfaf54920945549f1fd69a8810a830.

Article 19 (2019) Social media councils: Consultation. In: *Article 19*. Available at: www.article19.org/resources/social-media-councils-consultation/.

Banchik AV (2020) Disappearing acts: Content moderation and emergent practices to preserve at-risk human rights–related content. *New Media & Society*. DOI: 10.1177/1461444820912724.

Barlow JP (1996) Declaration of the independence of cyberspace. Available at: www.eff.org/cyberspace-independence.

Bean R (2020) Is the business world ready for a chief data ethics officer? *Forbes*, 13 July. Available at: www.forbes.com/sites/ciocentral/2020/07/13/is-the-business-world-ready-for-a-chief-data-ethics-officer/.

Benkler Y, Faris R and Roberts H (2018) *Network Propaganda: Manipulation, Disinformation, and Radicalization in American Politics*. New York: Oxford University Press.

Bowers J and Zittrain J (2020) Answering impossible questions: Content governance in an age of disinformation. *Harvard Kennedy School Misinformation Review*. DOI: 10.37016/mr-2020-005.

Brkan M (2019) Artificial intelligence and democracy: The impact of disinformation, social bots and political targeting. *Delphi – Interdisciplinary Review of Emerging Technologies* 2(2): 66–71. DOI: 10.21552/delphi/2019/2/4.

Burgess J and Green J (2018) *YouTube: Online Video and Participatory Culture*. Second edition. Cambridge: Polity Press.

Calvano E and Polo M (2020) Market power, competition and innovation in digital markets: A survey. *Information Economics and Policy*. DOI: 10.1016/j.infoecopol.2020.100853.

Clegg N (2020) Welcoming the oversight board. In: *Facebook*. Available at: https://about.fb.com/news/2020/05/welcoming-the-oversight-board/.

Clinton H (2011) *Internet Rights and Wrongs: Choices and Challenges in a Networked World*. Washington, DC: US Department of State.

Covington P, Adams J and Sargin E (2016) Deep neural networks for YouTube recommendations. In: *Proceedings of the 10th ACM Conference on Recommender Systems*, Boston MA, USA, 7 September, pp. 191–198. ACM. DOI: 10.1145/2959100.2959190.

Digital, Culture, Media and Sport Committee (2019) *Disinformation and 'Fake News': Final Report*. 18 February. London: House of Commons.

Elvestad E and Phillips A (2018) *Misunderstanding News Audiences: Seven Myths of the Social Media Era*. London: Routledge.

ERGA (2020) *ERGA Report on disinformation: Assessment of the implementation of the Code of Practice*. Brussels: European Regulators Group for Audiovisual Media Services (ERGA).

European Commission (2018) *EU Code of Practice on Disinformation*. 26 September. Brussels: European Commission (c). Available at: https://ec.europa.eu/newsroom/dae/document.cfm?doc_id=54454.

European Commission (2020) *Assessment of the implementation of the Code of Practice on Disinformation*. 8 May. Luxembourg: European Commission.

Faddoul M, Chaslot G and Farid H (2020) A longitudinal analysis of YouTube's promotion of conspiracy videos. *arXiv:2003.03318 [cs]*. Available at: http://arxiv.org/abs/2003.03318.

Farkas J and Schou J (2019) *Post-Truth, Fake News and Democracy: Mapping the Politics of Falsehood*. Abingdon: Routledge.

Flew T, Martin F and Suzor N (2019) Internet regulation as media policy: Rethinking the question of digital communication platform governance. *Journal of Digital Media & Policy* 10(1): 33–50. DOI: 10.1386/jdmp.10.1.33_1.

Garfinkel S, Matthews J, Shapiro SS et al. (2017) Toward algorithmic transparency and accountability. *Communications of the ACM* 60(9): 5–5. DOI: 10.1145/3125780.

Gillespie T (2017) Algorithmically recognizable: Santorum's Google problem, and Google's Santorum problem. *Information, Communication and Society* 20(1): 63–80. DOI: 10.1080/1369118X.2016.1199721.

Gillespie T (2018) *Custodians of the Internet: Platforms, Content Moderation, and the Hidden Decisions that Shape Social Media.* New Haven: Yale University Press.

Global Disinformation Index (2019) *The Quarter Billion Dollar Question: How is Disinformation Gaming Ad Tech?* 4 September. London: Global Disinformation Index.

Global Disinformation Index (2020) *Why is ad tech paying US$25 million to Covid-19 DisInfo sites?* 8 July. London: Global Disinformation Index. Available at: https://disinformationindex.org/2020/07/why-is-ad-tech-paying-us25-million-to-covid-19-disinfo-sites/.

Golebiewski M and boyd d (2018) *Data Voids: Where Missing Data Can Easily Be Exploited.* New York: Data & Society.

Gordon BR, Zettelmeyer F, Bhargava N et al. (2017) A comparison of approaches to advertising measurement: Evidence from Big Field experiments at Facebook. *SSRN Electronic Journal.* DOI: 10.2139/ssrn.3033144.

Gorwa R (2019) The platform governance triangle: Conceptualising the informal regulation of online content. *Internet Policy Review* 8(2): 1–22. DOI: 10.14763/2019.2.1407.

Graham M (2019) The Trade Desk's new ad campaign pokes Google and Facebook in the ribs. *CNBC*, 23 September.

Hatmaker T (2020) Before buying Instagram, Zuckerberg warned employees of 'battle' to 'dislodge' competitor. *Tech Crunch*, 29 July. Available at: https://techcrunch.com/2020/07/29/facebook-instagram-deal-illegal-nadler/#:~:text=TechCrunch-,Before%20buying%20Instagram%2C%20 Zuckerberg%20warned%20employees%20of,battle'%20to%20'dislodge'%20 competitor&text=Nadler%20went%20on%20to%20declare,of%20 Instagram%20violated%20antitrust%20laws.

Hoffmann S, Taylor E and Bradshaw S (2019) *The market of disinformation.* Oxford: Oxford Technology and Elections Commission.

Hussein E, Juneja P and Mitra T (2020) Measuring misinformation in video search platforms: An audit study on YouTube. *Proceedings of the ACM on Human-Computer Interaction* 4(CSCW1): 1–27. DOI: 10.1145/3392854.

Ingram M (2020) Experts weigh in on Facebook's new Oversight Board. *Columbia Journalism Review*, 14 May. Available at: www.cjr.org/the_media_today/experts-weigh-in-on-facebooks-new-oversight-board.php.

Kaiser B (2019) *Targeted: The Cambridge Analytica Whistleblower's inside Story of How Big Data, Trump, and Facebook Broke Democracy and How It Can Happen Again.* Available at: www.overdrive.com/search?q=CA1FFF2C-21DF-44ED-BD19-7A8D62C53616.

Kaiser J and Rauchfleisch A (2019) The implications of venturing down the rabbit hole. In: *Internet Policy Review*. Available at: https://policyreview.info/articles/news/implications-venturing-down-rabbit-hole/1406.

Kaye D (2018) *A Human Rights Approach to Platform Content Regulation*. New York: United Nations.

Klein E (2018) Mark Zuckerberg on Facebook's hardest year, and what comes next. *Vox*, 2 April. Available at: www.vox.com/2018/4/2/17185052/mark-zuckerberg-facebook-interview-fake-news-bots-cambridge?utm_campaign=The%20Interface&utm_medium=email&utm_source=Revue%20newsletter.

Kosinski M, Stillwell D and Graepel T (2013) Private traits and attributes are predictable from digital records of human behavior. *Proceedings of the National Academy of Sciences* 110(15): 5802–5805. DOI: 10.1073/pnas.1218772110.

Kreiss D and McGregor SC (2019) The 'arbiters of what our voters see': Facebook and Google's struggle with policy, process, and enforcement around political advertising. *Political Communication* 36(4): 499–522. DOI: 10.1080/10584609.2019.1619639.

Langlois G and Elmer G (2013) The research politics of social media platforms. *Culture Machine* 14. Available at: https://culturemachine.net/platform-politics/.

Ledwich M and Zaitsev A (2019) Algorithmic extremism: Examining YouTube's rabbit hole of radicalization. *arXiv:1912.11211 [cs]*. Available at: http://arxiv.org/abs/1912.11211.

Lemoine L (2020) Competition law: Big Tech mergers, a dominance tool. In: *European Digital Rights*. Available at: https://edri.org/competition-law-big-tech-mergers-a-dominance-tool/.

Li H-Y, Bailey A, Huynh D et al. (2020) YouTube as a source of information on Covid-19: A pandemic of misinformation? *BMJ Global Health* 5(5). DOI: 10.1136/bmjgh-2020-002604.

Madrigal A and Meyer R (2018) How Facebook's chaotic push into video cost hundreds of journalists their jobs. *The Atlantic*, 18 October. Available at: www.theatlantic.com/technology/archive/2018/10/facebook-driven-video-push-may-have-cost-483-journalists-their-jobs/573403/.

Marsden C, Meyer T and Brown I (2020) Platform values and democratic elections: How can the law regulate digital disinformation? *Computer Law & Security Review* 36. DOI: 10.1016/j.clsr.2019.105373.

Marshall J (2014) WTF is real-time bidding? *Digiday*, 17 February. Available at: https://digiday.com/media/what-is-real-time-bidding/.

Morozov EV (2011) *The Net Delusion: The Dark Side of Internet Freedom*. First edition. New York: Public Affairs.

Nicholls R (2020) In a world first, Australia plans to force Facebook and Google to pay for news (but ABC and SBS miss out). *The Conversation*, 31 July. Available at: https://theconversation.com/in-a-world-first-australia-plans-to-force-facebook-and-google-to-pay-for-news-but-abc-and-sbs-miss-out-143740.

Nielsen RK (n.d.) Media capture in the digital age. In: Schiffrin A (ed.) *In the Service of Power: Media Capture and the Threat to Democracy*. Washington, DC: Centre for International Media, pp. 33–41.

Ovide S (2020) Big Tech's backlash is just starting. *The New York Times*, 30 July. Available at: www.nytimes.com/2020/07/30/technology/big-tech-backlash.html.

Pasquale F (2015) *The Black Box Society: The Secret Algorithms That Control Money and Information*. Cambridge, MA: Harvard University Press.

Plantin J-C and Punathambekar A (2019) Digital media infrastructures: pipes, platforms, and politics. *Media, Culture & Society* 41(2): 163–174. DOI: 10.1177/0163443718818376.

Prasad R (2018) Ascendant India, digital India: How net neutrality advocates defeated Facebook's Free Basics. *Media, Culture & Society* 40(3): 415–431. DOI: 10.1177/0163443717736117.

Ribeiro MH, Ottoni R, West R et al. (2019) Auditing radicalization pathways on YouTube. Available at: http://arxiv.org/abs/1908.08313.

Ryan J (2019) *Ryan's testimony at International Grand Chamber: RTB data breach enables disinformation. Enforcers can be sued*. 11 November. Dublin: Brave. Available at: https://brave.com/dr-johnny-ryans-testimony-at-the-international-grand-chamber-on-disinformation-and-fake-news/.

Santa Clara Principles (2018) The Santa Clara Principles On Transparency and Accountability in Content Moderation. Available at: https://santaclaraprinciples.org/.

Shah H (2018) Algorithmic accountability. *Philosophical Transactions of the Royal Society A: Mathematical, Physical and Engineering Sciences* 376(2128). DOI: 10.1098/rsta.2017.0362.

Solon O and Levin S (2016) How Google's search algorithm spreads false information with a rightwing bias. *The Guardian*, 16 December. Available at: www.theguardian.com/technology/2016/dec/16/google-autocomplete-rightwing-bias-algorithm-political-propaganda.

Solsman J (2018) YouTube's AI is the puppet master over most of what you watch. *CNET*, 10 January. Available at: www.cnet.com/news/youtube-ces-2018-neal-mohan/.

Stiglitz J (2017) Toward a taxonomy of media capture. In: Schiffrin A (ed.) *In the Service of Power: Media Capture and the Threat to Democracy*. Washington, DC: Centre for International Media, p. 9018.

Tassi P (2020) Microsoft and Sony are suspending Facebook advertising, But it's less noble than it sounds. *Forbes*, 4 July. Available at: www.forbes.com/sites/paultassi/2020/07/04/microsoft-and-sony-are-suspending-facebook-advertising-but-its-less-noble-than-it-sounds/#7b66aa671dca.

Tobin A (2019) HUD sues Facebook over housing discrimination and says the company's algorithms have made the problem worse. *ProPublica*, March. Available at: www.propublica.org/article/hud-sues-facebook-housing-discrimination-advertising-algorithms.

Tromble R and McGregor SC (2019) You break it, you buy it: The naiveté of social engineering in tech – and how to fix it. *Political Communication* 36(2): 324–332. DOI: 10.1080/10584609.2019.1609860.

Tufekci Z (2018) YouTube the great radicaliser. *The New York Times*, 10 March. Available at: www.nytimes.com/2018/03/10/opinion/sunday/youtube-politics-radical.html.

Turner Lee N, Resnick P and Barton G (2019) *Algorithmic Bias Detection and Mitigation: Best Practices and Policies to Reduce Consumer Harms*. 22 May. Washington, DC: Brookings Institution. Available at: www.brookings.edu/research/algorithmic-bias-detection-and-mitigation-best-practices-and-policies-to-reduce-consumer-harms/.

Veale M, Van Kleek M and Binns R (2018) Fairness and accountability design needs for algorithmic support in high-stakes public sector decision-making. In: *Proceedings of the 2018 CHI Conference on Human Factors in Computing Systems – CHI '18*. Montreal: ACM Press, pp. 1–14. DOI: 10.1145/3173574.3174014.

Wilson M (2017) Algorithms (and the) everyday. *Information, Communication and Society* 20(1): 137–150. DOI: 10.1080/1369118X.2016.1200645.

Wolde HT and Auchard E (2014) Germany's top publisher bows to Google in news licensing row. *Reuters*, 5 November. Available at: www.reuters.com/article/us-google-axel-sprngr/germanys-top-publisher-bows-to-google-in-news-licensing-row-idUSKBN0IP1YT20141105.

Wong JC and Levin S (2019) YouTube vows to recommend fewer conspiracy theory videos. *The Guardian*, 25 January. Available at: www.theguardian.com/technology/2019/jan/25/youtube-conspiracy-theory-videos-recommendations.

Wu T (2017) Blind spot: The attention economy and the law. *Antitrust Law Journal* 82: 771–806.

YouTube (2019) Our ongoing work to tackle hate. In: *YouTube*. Available at: https://blog.youtube/news-and-events/our-ongoing-work-to-tackle-hate.

YouTube (2020) YouTube for the Press. In: *YouTube*. Available at: www.youtube.com/intl/en-GB/about/press/.

Zhao Z, Hong L, Wei L et al. (2019) Recommending what video to watch next: a multitask ranking system. In: *Proceedings of the 13th ACM Conference on Recommender Systems*. Copenhagen, 10 September, pp. 43–51. ACM. DOI: 10.1145/3298689.3346997.

Zuboff S (2019) Surveillance capitalism and the challenge of collective action. *New Labor Forum* 28(1): 10–29. DOI: 10.1177/1095796018819461.

4   Audiences

The ideal of an informed citizen underpins much scholarly research on democratic participation and the public communication of science. It is taken as a given that people should be informed about the major political issues of the day and about the scientific consensus on topics such as climate change, evolution, and the safety of vaccines. Yet, in each of these areas, there are striking gaps between public understanding and the body of available evidence (Lewandowsky et al. 2017). As the news media played a dominant role in informing audiences over the past century, it has been subject to extensive criticism for misleading the public through inadequate or sensational reporting (Altheide 1976). This is perhaps best exemplified by coverage of climate change, which manufactured artificial debates about the scientific evidence (Timm et al. 2020).

With the advent of digital media, journalists lost their monopoly over public information and new concerns emerged around misinformed digital audiences. Much of this hinged on the idea that personalisation algorithms generate information 'filter bubbles' (Pariser 2012) that are skewed to one's existing biases. A distinct, but related, idea contends that digital platforms allow people to isolate themselves in 'echo chambers' of like-minded individuals (Sunstein 2011). Both of these concepts are frequently invoked in policy and media discussions of disinformation. Although researchers have found evidence for filter bubble effects in recommendation algorithms (Hussein et al. 2020), there is an important distinction between filter bubbles on specific platforms like YouTube and the totality of information sources people consume. In this regard, empirical studies indicate that people's information diets are generally quite varied, which may offset the filter bubble effects of specific platforms (Flaxman et al. 2016; Guess et al. 2018). Yet, the ubiquity of references to filter bubbles and echo chambers in popular debates about disinformation generates a moral panic about digital media and audience vulnerabilities (see Bruns 2019).

The disconnect between data availability and audience practices can also generate false perceptions of the problem. For example, disinformation on Twitter is widely studied because it is relatively easy to access the data, but Twitter is far less popular among audiences than Facebook or YouTube (Perrin and Anderson 2019). Considering the global perspective, there are pronounced differences in technology use and audience consumption trends. For example, in the Global North WhatsApp is primarily used to send messages among small groups of peers and is just one of many platforms used on a daily basis. In contrast, WhatsApp and similar platforms are a key driver of internet uptake across much of the Global South where internet connections are unreliable and data costs are high (Marcus and Wong 2016). In these countries, WhatsApp is more akin to broadcasting with large-scale participation in groups defined by a common interest rather than any personal relationships (Mahapatra and Plagemann 2019).

As outlined in Chapter 2, there is ample evidence for the prevalence of manipulative content. Yet, some empirical studies find that audience exposure to disinformation is far less widespread than initially speculated (Allcott and Gentzkow 2017; Guess et al. 2020). However, it should be noted that these studies focused on a set of fake news articles and websites surrounding the 2016 US presidential election. Yet, manipulative content often falls outside the narrow definition of 'fake news' (Marwick and Lewis 2017) while recent work on Covid-19 finds that audiences reported high levels of exposure to disinformation (Hameleers et al. 2020). What this underscores is the dynamic nature of the disinformation environment and the need to understand audiences in specific contexts. Findings from one country, time-period, or topic domain do not necessarily translate to other contexts.

To that end, a key aim of this chapter is to move beyond simplistic ideas of audience vulnerability to advance a more nuanced understanding of the complex overlap of factors that shape audience engagement with online disinformation. We examine how individual scenarios of disinformation are shaped by psychological factors including the cognitive biases that influence engagement with information; the technological basis of digital media consumption; and, of course, the political and social contexts of particular audiences including their perceptions of news and journalism. The confluence of these factors is then explored through a case study of vaccine hesitancy and anti-vax disinformation.

Understanding susceptibility to disinformation

In what follows, we outline what research in cognitive psychology, political communication, and related fields have established about susceptibility to disinformation. A concerted effort to understand susceptibility to online disinformation is in its infancy, but researchers have been investigating how people process online information and assess its credibility for many decades (Flanagin et al. 2020; Metzger et al. 2010). The collective insights from this work may be summarised in terms of the factors that influence how individuals evaluate information generally and in online environments specifically.

Cognitive ability and attention: Cognitive ability refers to a person's capabilities for reasoning and problem solving. Studies indicate that people with low cognitive ability are more susceptible to disinformation and more resistant to its correction (De keersmaecker and Roets 2017); most likely because they have a weaker capacity to filter out irrelevant information and are less likely to have developed effective strategies for evaluating information. As cognitive ability is typically lower among children and the elderly, these cohorts may be more susceptible to false information (Guess et al. 2020). A related concept, need-for-cognition, refers to a person's predisposition to seek out or enjoy analytical thinking. Those who are predisposed to analytical thinking are therefore more likely to interrogate information rather than accept it uncritically. Based on a series of experimental studies, Pennycook and Rand (2019) suggest that a low level of analytical thinking is a key factor influencing susceptibility to disinformation; overriding the other factors discussed below such as an individual's level of prior knowledge or partisan bias.

While cognitive ability and need for cognition refer to relatively stable traits, there is also a situational dimension. In everyday scenarios, people frequently lack the time and inclination to devote their full attention to processing new information. In digital environments, this is compounded by media multitasking (Moisala et al. 2016) and the incessant competition for attention from various media and information sources (Weng et al. 2013). Faced with a constant flow of new information from multiple sources, people often only skim content and, in these circumstances, attention-grabbing or emotionally loaded content can override judgement. Distracted attention is why so many of us are easily fooled by trick questions even though we have the cognitive ability to work out the correct answer. Consider the following: if you're running a race and you pass the person in second place, what place are you in? The correct answer is second place, but arriving at this answer requires paying close attention to the question. When people only process the gist of the question, the intuitive answer seems to be first place. To counteract this, one promising area of research finds that simply prompting people to think about the accuracy of a message greatly improves their ability to reject disinformation (Pennycook et al. 2018).

As discussed in the preceding chapter, platform algorithms and engagement metrics underpin an 'attention economy' (Wu 2017). The drive for audience attention pushed some online news organisations towards a click-bait strategy that prioritised sensational headlines and stories (Myllylahti 2020). This strategy is often replicated in the fake news genre of disinformation as evidenced by this infamous headline from the 2016 US presidential election: 'Pope Francis Shocks World, Endorses Donald Trump For President'. An analysis by *Buzzfeed* (Silverman 2016) found that fake stories like this generated more engagement on Facebook than news stories from major media outlets. However, we cannot infer from this that people afforded any credibility to these fake stories as engagement metrics alone offer no indication of belief, motivation, or interest. For example, a UK study found that people are motivated to share news stories for a variety of reasons including a desire to express opinions, to provoke discussion, and to inform or entertain others (Chadwick and Vaccari 2019).

Bias, knowledge, and familiarity: As noted above, the incessant flow of updates on social media platforms places a high cognitive burden on the individual. To navigate these rich information environments, individuals may be guided by cognitive biases and heuristics that help reduce the burden and minimise feelings of cognitive dissonance. Here, we discuss two cognitive biases: confirmation bias and motivated reasoning. Confirmation bias refers to an implicit tendency to pay attention to information that is consistent with preexisting beliefs while ignoring or rejecting information that counters those beliefs (Knobloch-Westerwick et al. 2017). Similarly, motivated reasoning concerns the tendency to readily accept new information that is congruent with preexisting beliefs and to critically analyse information that contradicts those beliefs (Kahan 2012). Both biases can leave individuals poorly placed to recognise and reject disinformation (Kahan 2017). However, despite the popular appeal of these concepts in policy and media discussions about disinformation, experimental studies by Pennycook and Rand (2019) indicate that susceptibility to disinformation may be driven by a circumstantial failure to apply analytical reasoning rather than any ingrained partisan bias.

Nevertheless, prior knowledge appears to play an important role in susceptibility to disinformation because people draw on what they already know to process new information. For any given topic, an individual may be informed, uninformed, or misinformed to varying degrees. Some studies have found that because exposure to news and information on social media is often incidental rather than actively sought out, people may believe they are well informed without engaging with the news in any meaningful way (Boczkowski et al. 2018; Gil de Zúñiga and Diehl 2019). While the uninformed simply lack knowledge, the misinformed have incorrect knowledge, which they believe is true. Naturally, this has knock-on implications for how these individuals respond to disinformation. Among a nationally representative sample of French, German and US adults, Fernbach et al. (2019) found that individuals with a strong opposition to gene therapies and genetically modified (GM) foods had low levels of objective knowledge, but a high perception of their own scientific understanding. In other words, they assumed knowledge they did not have and this generated a false confidence in their ability to evaluate complex evidence. In this case, the misinformed individuals were motivated by their ideological opposition to the science, but familiarity with false claims can also lead to inaccurate judgements.

A significant body of research affirms that incorrect information seems more reliable if it is familiar. This phenomenon, known as the illusory truth effect, is linked to memory as familiar information is more easily recalled and appears more reliable as a result (Hasher et al. 1977). Thus, when people are repeatedly exposed to online disinformation, those claims enter memory and can gain credibility through repetition over time. This effect appears to hold true regardless of an individual's cognitive ability or need for cognition (De keersmaecker et al. 2020) and regardless of an individual's knowledge about the subject (Fazio et al. 2015). Even when false information is corrected, it can leave 'belief echoes' that continue to affect attitudes (Wood and Porter 2019). This has major implications for disinformation fact-checks and corrections because it implies that the repetition of false claims can potentially confuse audiences. On this basis, best-practice recommends that journalists and fact-checkers avoid giving unnecessary oxygen to incorrect information (Wardle 2018). A related idea holds that fact-checks and debunks can potentially backfire by reinforcing false beliefs (Berinsky 2017). However, researchers have largely disregarded the backfire effect as a 'zombie theory' (Porter and Wood 2020). Yet, it is still cited by the platforms – especially Facebook – as a reason to avoid fact-checking content (ibid.).

Emotional triggers and peer groups: Throughout history, propagandists have provoked fear and anger to garner support for causes and to demonise out groups. This strategy is often replicated in online disinformation (Paschen 2019) as content that triggers negative emotions influences judgement (Weeks 2015) and is more likely to go viral (Vosoughi et al. 2018). For example, a US study examining polarised issues such as gun control and same-sex marriage found that the use of emotional language increased the diffusion of political messages within the polarised groups (Brady et al. 2017). By triggering emotions, bad actors can enlist audiences to do the work of propagating disinformation. Triggering fear and anger appears to be particularly effective. By appealing to people's fears, hoaxes such as the 2018 'Momo challenge' generated viral panic (see Magid 2018). In this case, the hoax alleged that an online video was provoking children to self-harm, prompting authorities from Mexico to Pakistan to issue warnings to the public. Crucially, the motivation to share a fear-based hoax may be independent of whether people believe it. When faced with a grave claim about a threat to children – and one set against wider concerns about children's use of digital media – it seems that many people opted to share the story 'just in case' it was true (ibid.).

Audience studies provide insight into this process. In their report on attitudes to disinformation in Kenya and Nigeria, Chakrabarti et al. (2018) found that a sense of civic duty motivated people to share disinformation; especially when the disinformation concerned issues of personal safety and security. Importantly, the authors note that the desire to behave in a civic way (i.e. informing others of potential danger) was superseded by a desire to gain social recognition (i.e. being the first to share the information). As such, the instinct to share was privileged over the instinct to verify. Finding ways to reverse these instincts – whether through education, media and information literacy, or technological interventions – would seem to be a key priority for countering the spread of disinformation. Of course, it is a mistake to assume that such countermeasures will be sufficient to offset deep-seated biases. In India, Banaji and Bhat (2019) also found that a sense of civic duty fuelled the spread of unverified rumours about crimes attributed to minorities. However, the authors also note that social and political inequalities, rather than technology, are the essence of the problem (see Chapter 2).

Pathologising audiences

While acknowledging that certain traits and circumstances make individuals more susceptible to disinformation, there is clearly a danger of oversimplifying disinformation audiences. As Chakravartty and Roy

(2017) argue, the media and policy discussions surrounding disinformation has revived the 'hypodermic needle' model of media effects. Popular
in early twentieth-century studies of propaganda, the hypodermic
needle model assumes that audiences are passive recipients of media
messages and therefore highly vulnerable to manipulation. In contrast,
Wardle and Derakshan (2017) advocate the 'circuit of culture' tradition
as a means to analyse disinformation. This tradition emphasises the
interrelationships between producers, texts, and audiences and, consequently, treats audiences as active interpreters of disinformation rather
than passive recipients of manipulative messages.

In the wake of Brexit and the 2016 US presidential election, a
number of studies reinforced the 'hypodermic needle' view of deficient
audiences. In a widely-reported study of US students, Wineburg et al.
(2016) found that the vast majority were unable to differentiate a news
story from sponsored content and unable to detect bias in corporate
and political messages. Similarly, a representative YouGov survey asked
1,684 UK adults to evaluate six news articles among which there were
three disinformation items (Channel 4 2017). Only 4 per cent correctly
evaluated all the articles while almost half believed at least one disinformation article was true. Studies like these are often used to emphasise the need to invest in media literacy education and in the emerging
field of news literacy (see Chapter 5). However, echoing Bruns' (2019)
concern about the moral panic surrounding filter bubbles, there is a
danger of blaming audience deficiencies without attending to the actual
perspectives of audiences or to the wider social and political dimensions
of the problem.

In general, audiences appear to have an ambiguous understanding
of disinformation. Despite the extensive media coverage devoted to
fake news and Russian disinformation, audience perceptions are at
odds with the way academics, journalists, and policymakers typically
think about the problem. In an analysis of audience perspectives in four
countries (Finland, Spain, UK, and US), Nielsen and Graves (2017)
found that people perceived the differences between fake news and
mainstream news in terms of degrees. When asked to provide examples
of fake news, they cited poor journalism, propaganda, and advertising
more frequently than fake stories in the guise of news reports. The most
recent Reuters Institute Digital News Report (Newman et al. 2020), a
study of news consumption and attitudes across 40 countries, found
that audiences were primarily concerned about disinformation eman-
ating from domestic politicians rather than foreign bad actors. In the
US, those who identified as right-wing were more likely to highlight the
news media as a source of disinformation.

A similar gap in understanding is evident in perceptions of news. While academics, journalists, and policymakers utilise a relatively stable (and perhaps idealised) concept of news media as a fourth estate (Hampton 2010), audience perspectives are more fluid. Rather than predefined ideas about the democratic function of news, audiences 'assemble their news diets and news repertoires in contexts of everyday life' (Schrøder 2015: 61). Moreover, everyday life is lived in a multi-platform hybrid media environment in which the boundaries between different media genres and information sources are fuzzy. In a study investigating how audiences perceive the blending of news and entertainment formats, Edgerly and Vraga (2019: 821) found that 'modern media consumers see little systematic distinction in news-ness between "legacy" media sources and "newer" ideologically voiced, media sources'. Yet, this distinction underpins much research on disinformation. The ambiguities evident in audiences' understanding of what counts as news and disinformation have important implications. As outlined in Chapter 5, current efforts to build algorithmic detection tools for disinformation draw on datasets that apply narrow definitions of disinformation and news (Torabi Asr and Taboada 2019). Consequently, when these algorithms 'predict' disinformation, it is very possible that audiences will question the results.

As audience attitudes towards disinformation appear to be closely entwined with their attitudes towards journalism, it is important to consider a broader set of trends. Many studies have affirmed a growing distrust of news media (see Fenton 2019) along with a decline in perceptions of news media quality (Wagner and Boczkowski 2019) and increased cynicism about journalism (Tsang 2020). Media cynicism is encouraged by actors on the right and left (Figenschou and Ihlebæk 2019) including elite actors who denigrate professional journalism as 'fake news'. However, journalism scandals and biases in coverage are also contributory factors. As Fenton (2019: 38) argues, 'until journalism is able to hold its own institutions of power to account, expose its own malpractices and is willing to challenge some of the most obvious abuses of media power, distrust in news journalism is likely to grow'. Quite apart from tabloid hysteria and malpractice, one obvious example is the complicity of many quality news outlets in the US and the UK in disseminating false claims in support for the 2003 invasion of Iraq (Dimaggio 2012). Thus, if audiences need to gain media literacy skills to recognise quality journalism, the news media also need to find ways to earn and maintain public trust.

While much of the literature on audience susceptibility to disinformation focuses on individual traits and the need to upskill audiences, a broader perspective examines the characteristics of media and political systems. To understand national levels of resilience to online disinformation, Humprecht et al. (2020) conducted a comparative analysis of 18 countries across Europe and North America. To do so, they constructed predictors based on characteristics that limit resilience within the media environment (e.g. low trust in news, weak public service media); the political environment (e.g. populism, social polarisation); and the economic environment (e.g. large advertising markets, high social media use). Based on these characteristics, Canada along with Northern and Western European countries appeared to have a much higher resilience than Southern Europe. The US emerged as an outlier as 'its peculiar contextual conditions make it a unique case' (Humprecht et al. 2020: 508). This perspective potentially shifts the focus from protecting vulnerable audiences to improving and reinforcing the democratic qualities of political and media systems; a theme we take up in Chapter 6.

Case study: anti-vaccine disinformation

Countries across the world have experienced a dramatic increase in outbreaks of vaccine-preventable diseases (WHO 2019). Many studies link vaccine hesitancy to digital media consumption (Martin and Petrie 2017; Stecula et al. 2020) and to social media where anti-vaccine disinformation is prevalent (RSPH 2019). Anti-vaccine disinformation is varied as it targets different vaccines, countries, and cultures. Broadly, this disinformation claims that vaccines contain harmful toxins; cause illnesses; can be delayed without risk; and are less safe than gaining immunity through disease contraction (Smith 2017). Although it is difficult to measure the influence of this disinformation, even a small effect can have a major impact by undermining herd immunity. Unsurprisingly, the Covid-19 pandemic emboldened anti-vaccine activists and saw the emergence of new vaccine conspiracy theories (Hotez 2020).

While concerns about vaccine safety are as old as vaccines, the anti-vaccine movement in the Global North emerged in the 1990s when Andrew Wakefield published a (since-retracted) paper linking the MMR vaccine to autism. Around the same time, the advent of the web provided new opportunities for anti-vaccine activists to question the medical consensus (Kata 2012). A recent US study found that the majority of English language, anti-vaccine adverts on Facebook were funded by just two organisations: Stop Mandatory Vaccination and The World Mercury Project (Jamison et al. 2020). In addition, Russian trolls have attempted to fuel polarisation by simultaneously propagating pro-vaccine and anti-vaccine messages (Broniatowski et al. 2018). Apart from these bad actors, concerned parents spread false information among their peers (Tangherlini et al. 2016).

Amid mounting pressure, the platforms moved to curb the visibility of vaccine disinformation in 2019. Foreshadowing the response to Covid-19 a year later, the platforms blocked anti-vaccine hashtags and phrases, promoted authoritative information sources, and attempted to limit advertising for anti-vaccine content (Funke et al. 2019). In response, anti-vaccine activists adopted new tactics (Funke et al. 2019; Hotex 2020). For example, they employed less explicit terms such as #LearnTheRisk and #JustAsking and co-opted the #RightToChoose language of abortion rights (Funke 2020).

While there is ample evidence for the proliferation of anti-vaccine disinformation, the link to audience attitudes and behaviours is not well understood. Vaccine hesitancy encompasses a broad spectrum of attitudes from general concerns about the safety of vaccines to conspiratorial beliefs about the intentions of vaccination programmes. Within the literature, vaccine hesitancy is contextualised in terms of three broad factors: generational complacency, declining trust in medical expertise, and the influence of peers. Regarding complacency, an EU-wide study found that people aged under 65 tend to disregard the significance of vaccines (Larson et al. 2018). One explanation for this is that vaccines are victims of their own success (Smith 2017). Thanks to widespread vaccination, generations have grown up without a tangible awareness of the dangers of vaccine-preventable diseases.

Declining trust is often linked to the rise of a 'postmodern medical paradigm' whereby medical expertise is bypassed or dismissed (Kata 2012: 3778). A large US study found that low levels of trust in medical authorities is correlated with belief in vaccine disinformation regardless of differences in demographics and political partisanship (Stecula et al. 2020). Yet, issues of trust do have important political and historical contexts. For example, the history of covert, medical experimentation on African Americans makes disinformation about vaccines a plausible consideration for that community (Washington 2006). Similarly, the CIA's use of a fake vaccination programme to target Osama bin Laden contributed to a vaccine backlash in Pakistan as it appeared to vindicate a long-standing conspiracy theory about the nefarious intentions of international vaccination programmes (Bhattacharjee and Dotto 2020). In other instances, low trust in medical experts emerges from personal experiences, which can drive parents to become advocates against vaccines. An anthropological study of a parent-led campaign against the HPV vaccine in Ireland found that parents were incentivised to organise and form links with groups abroad due to a perceived lack of satisfactory engagement with their own doctors (Drazkiewicz 2020).

The academic medical community also bears some responsibility for the problem. Wakefield's autism study was published in one of the most prestigious medical journals, *The Lancet*, but the paper was not retracted until 2010, 12 years after its publication. Bowing to pressure, from anti-vaccine actors, health authorities phased out the use of a mercury-based preservative (thimerosal) even though there is no evidence linking this ingredient to autism (Mandavilli 20017). These actions have provided validation for anti-vaccine activists and clearly send confusing signals about safety to the public.

As noted above, a sense of civic duty can inspire people to share disinformation and to re-upload content that has been removed from the platforms (Bhattacharjee and Dotto 2020). The testimony of parents reporting negative experiences is particularly insidious because disinformation is spread by trusted peers and is accompanied by persuasive and personal storytelling (Tangherlini et al. 2016). While false claims about toxins and herd immunity may be countered with correct information, it is difficult to refute or contest claims about personal experience; not least because doing so is also socially taboo. Organisations like Stop Mandatory Vaccination exploit this by creating campaigns that emphasise the emotional testimony of parents who claim their children died or developed severe disabilities as a result of vaccination.

Studies indicate that anti-vaccine beliefs are tenacious and have not shifted substantially following major public awareness campaigns (Stecula et al. 2020). Relatedly, studies investigating how to correct vaccine disinformation find that presenting scientific evidence does little to challenge established views (Nyhan and Reifler 2015). Vaccines are an illustrative case of the dangers of disinformation and the challenges of countering it. While the infrastructure of online platforms enables anti-vaccine activists to target emotive messages at a large audience, it is clear that countering vaccine disinformation requires more than stemming the flow of online messages.

Conclusion

This chapter has parsed the factors that may influence audience susceptibility to disinformation, but it is important to recognise that these factors do not operate in isolation from each other. The confluence of overlapping factors makes it difficult to determine how disinformation influences audiences and in what circumstances. For their part, audiences appear to be concerned about exposure to disinformation and their ability to detect it. In 2019, the Reuters Digital News Report found that more than half of respondents expressed concerned about disinformation (Newman et al. 2019). Many respondents also reported changing their behaviour by checking the accuracy of news against other sources (41%) or declining to share a 'dubious' article (29%). While these self-reported trends seem positive, they raise further questions about what audiences consider dubious and how they make such evaluations.

In recent years, there has been a large volume of social network analyses on the diffusion of disinformation as well as surveys on audience attitudes and experiments on the effectiveness of interventions. In contrast, there is a dearth of ethnographic research on audience perceptions of disinformation. While survey and experimental designs are vital to understand broad patterns, they typically lack the detail and depth that can be achieved through ethnographic studies of specific audiences. To avoid a crude pathologisation of audiences, much work needs to be done to better understand the interpretative contexts of specific audiences. More generally, multiple types of quantitative and qualitative research are crucial to advance an understanding of disinformation, its influence, and its potential mitigation.

References

Allcott H and Gentzkow M (2017) Social media and fake news in the 2016 election. *Journal of Economic Perspectives* 31(2): 211–236. DOI: 10.1257/jep.31.2.211.

Altheide DL (1976) *Creating Reality: How TV News Distorts Events*. Beverly Hills: Sage.

Banaji S and Bhat R (2019) *WhatsApp Vigilantes: An Exploration of Citizen Reception and Circulation of WhatsApp Misinformation Linked to Mob Violence in India*. London: London School of Economics. Available at: http://eprints.lse.ac.uk/104316/1/Banaji_whatsapp_vigilantes_exploration_of_citizen_reception_published.pdf.

Berinsky AJ (2017) Rumors and health care reform: Experiments in political misinformation. *British Journal of Political Science* 47(2): 241–262. DOI: 10.1017/S0007123415000186.

Boczkowski PJ, Matassi M and Mitchelstein E (2018) How young users deal with multiple platforms: The role of meaning-making in social media repertoires. *Journal of Computer-Mediated Communication* 23(5): 245–259. DOI: 10.1093/jcmc/zmy012.

Brady WJ, Wills JA, Jost JT et al. (2017) Emotion shapes the diffusion of moralized content in social networks. *Proceedings of the National Academy of Sciences* 114(28): 7313–7318. DOI: 10.1073/pnas.1618923114.

Broniatowski DA, Jamison AM, Qi S et al. (2018) Weaponized health communication: Twitter bots and Russian trolls amplify the vaccine debate. *American Journal of Public Health* 108(10): 1378–1384. DOI: 10.2105/AJPH.2018.304567.

Bruns A (2019) *Are Filter Bubbles Real?* Digital futures. Cambridge, UK; Medford, MA: Polity Press.

Chadwick A and Vaccari C (2019) *News Sharing on UK Social Media: Misinformation, Disinformation and Correction.* Loughborough: Online Civic Culture Centre.

Chakrabarti S, Rooney C and Kweon M (n.d.) *Verification, Duty, Credibility: Fake News and Ordinary Citizens in Kenya and Nigeria.* London: BBC World Service. Available at: https://downloads.bbc.co.uk/mediacentre/bbc-fake-news-research-paper-nigeria-kenya.pdf.

Chakravartty P and Roy S (2017) Mediatized populisms: Inter-Asian lineages. *International Journal of Communication* 11: 4073–4092.

Channel 4 (2017) C4 study reveals only 4% surveyed can identify true or fake news. *Channel 4*, 2 June. Available at: www.channel4.com/press/news/c4-study-reveals-only-4-surveyed-can-identify-true-or-fake-news.

De Keersmaecker J and Roets A (2017) 'Fake news': Incorrect, but hard to correct. The role of cognitive ability on the impact of false information on social impressions. *Intelligence* 65: 107–110. DOI: 10.1016/j.intell.2017.10.005.

Dimaggio AR (2012) *When Media Goes to War Hegemonic Discourse, Public Opinion, and the Limits of Dissent.* New York: Aakar Books.

Drazkiewicz E (2019) When the truth is not all that matters: understanding trajectories of conspiracy theories in conflicts over vaccinations. *What Do We Do About Conspiracy Theories?* Maynooth: Maynooth University.

Edgerly S and Vraga EK (2019) News, entertainment, or both? Exploring audience perceptions of media genre in a hybrid media environment. *Journalism* 20(6): 807–826. DOI: 10.1177/1464884917730709.

Fazio LK, Brashier NM, Payne BK et al. (2015) Knowledge does not protect against illusory truth. *Journal of Experimental Psychology: General* 144(5): 993–1002. DOI: 10.1037/xge0000098.

Fenton N (2019) (Dis)Trust. *Journalism* 20(1): 36–39. DOI: 10.1177/1464884918807068.

Fernbach PM, Light N, Scott SE et al. (2019) Extreme opponents of genetically modified foods know the least but think they know the most. *Nature Human Behaviour* 3(3): 251–256. DOI: 10.1038/s41562-018-0520-3.

Figenschou TU and Ihlebæk KA (2019) Challenging journalistic authority: Media criticism in far-right alternative media. *Journalism Studies* 20(9): 1221–1237. DOI: 10.1080/1461670X.2018.1500868.

Flanagin AJ, Winter S and Metzger MJ (2020) Making sense of credibility in complex information environments: The role of message sidedness, information source, and thinking styles in credibility evaluation online. *Information, Communication and Society* 23(7): 1038–1056. DOI: 10.1080/1369118X.2018.1547411.

Flaxman S, Goel S and Rao JM (2016) Filter bubbles, echo chambers, and online news consumption. *Public Opinion Quarterly* 80(S1): 298–320. DOI: 10.1093/poq/nfw006.

Funke D, Benkelman S and Tardáguila C (2019) Anti-vaxxers are adopting new tactics. *Poynter*, 12 December. Available at: www.poynter.org/fact-checking/2019/anti-vaxxers-adopt-new-manipulation-tactics-to-spread-misinformation/.

Gil de Zúñiga H and Diehl T (2019) News finds me perception and democracy: Effects on political knowledge, political interest, and voting. *New Media & Society* 21(6): 1253–1271. DOI: 10.1177/1461444818817548.

Guess AM, Nyhan B, Lyons B et al. (2018) *Avoiding the Echo Chamber About Echo Chambers*. Miami: Knight Foundation.

Guess AM, Nyhan B and Reifler J (2020) Exposure to untrustworthy websites in the 2016 US election. *Nature Human Behaviour* 4(5): 472–480. DOI: 10.1038/s41562-020-0833-x.

Hameleers M, van der Meer TGLA and Brosius A (2020) Feeling 'disinformed' lowers compliance with Covid-19 guidelines: Evidence from the US, UK, Netherlands and Germany. *Harvard Kennedy School Misinformation Review*. DOI: 10.37016/mr-2020-023.

Hampton M (2010) The fourth estate ideal in journalism history. In: Allan S (ed.) *The Routledge Companion to News and Journalism*. New York: Routledge, pp. 3–12.

Hasher L, Goldstein D and Toppino T (1977) Frequency and the conference of referential validity. *Journal of Verbal Learning and Verbal Behavior* 16(1): 107–112. DOI: 10.1016/S0022-5371(77)80012-1.

Hotez PJ (2020) Covid-19 meets the antivaccine movement. *Microbes and Infection* 22(4–5): 162–164. DOI: 10.1016/j.micinf.2020.05.010.

Humprecht E, Esser F and Van Aelst P (2020) Resilience to online disinformation: A framework for cross-national comparative research. *The International Journal of Press/Politics*. DOI: 10.1177/1940161219900126.

Hussein E, Juneja P and Mitra T (2020) Measuring misinformation in video search platforms: An audit study on YouTube. *Proceedings of the ACM on Human-Computer Interaction* 4(CSCW1): 1–27. DOI: 10.1145/3392854.

Jamison AM, Broniatowski DA, Dredze M et al. (2020) Vaccine-related advertising in the Facebook Ad Archive. *Vaccine* 38(3): 512–520. DOI: 10.1016/j.vaccine.2019.10.066.

Jankowski NW (2018) Researching fake news: A selective examination of empirical studies. *Javnost – The Public* 25(1–2): 248–255. DOI: 10.1080/13183222.2018.1418964.

Kahan DM (2012) Ideology, motivated reasoning, and cognitive reflection: An experimental study. *SSRN Electronic Journal*. DOI: 10.2139/ssrn.2182588.

Kahan DM (2017) Misconceptions, misinformation, and the logic of identity-protective cognition. *SSRN Electronic Journal.* DOI: 10.2139/ssrn.2973067.

Kata A (2012) Anti-vaccine activists, Web 2.0, and the postmodern paradigm – An overview of tactics and tropes used online by the anti-vaccination movement. *Vaccine* 30(25): 3778–3789. DOI: 10.1016/j.vaccine.2011.11.112.

Knobloch-Westerwick S, Mothes C and Polavin N (2017) Confirmation bias, ingroup bias, and negativity bias in selective exposure to political information. *Communication Research* 47(1): 104–124. DOI: 10.1177/0093650217719596.

Larson H, de Figueiredo A, Karafillakis E et al. (2018) *State of Vaccine Confidence in the EU.* Luxembourg: European Commission.

Lewandowsky S, Ecker UKH and Cook J (2017) Beyond misinformation: Understanding and coping with the 'post-truth' era. *Journal of Applied Research in Memory and Cognition* 6(4): 353–369. DOI: 10.1016/j.jarmac.2017.07.008.

Magid L (2018) Dire warnings about children dying because of apps and games are a form of 'juvenoia'. In: *London School of Economics.* Available at: https://blogs.lse.ac.uk/parenting4digitalfuture/2018/09/21/dire-warnings-about-children-dying-because-of-apps-and-games-are-a-form-of-juvenoia/.

Mahapatra S and Plagemann J (2019) *Polarisation and Politicisation: The Social Media Strategies of Indian Political Parties.* Hamburg: German Institute of Global and Area Studies. Available at: https://nbn-resolving.org/urn:nbn:de:0168-ssoar-61811–8.

Mandavilli A (2007) Unreasonable doubt. *Nature*, 15 June. Available at: www.nature.com/news/2007/070615/full/news070611-13.html.

Marcus A and Wong A (2016) *Internet for All: A Framework for Accelerating Internet Access and Adoption.* 12 May. Geneva: World Economic Forum.

Martin LR and Petrie KJ (2017) Understanding the dimensions of anti-vaccination attitudes: The Vaccination Attitudes Examination (VAX) Scale. *Annals of Behavioral Medicine* 51(5): 652–660. DOI: 10.1007/s12160-017-9888-y.

Marwick A and Lewis R (2017) *Media Manipulation and Disinformation Online.* New York: Data & Society.

Metzger MJ, Flanagin AJ and Medders RB (2010) Social and heuristic approaches to credibility evaluation online. *Journal of Communication* 60(3): 413–439. DOI: 10.1111/j.1460-2466.2010.01488.x.

Moisala M, Salmela V, Hietajärvi L et al. (2016) Media multitasking is associated with distractibility and increased prefrontal activity in adolescents and young adults. *NeuroImage* 134: 113–121. DOI: 10.1016/j.neuroimage.2016.04.011.

Myllylahti M (2020) Paying attention to attention: A conceptual framework for studying news reader revenue models related to platforms. *Digital Journalism* 8(5): 567–575. DOI: 10.1080/21670811.2019.1691926.

Newman N, Fletcher R, Kalogeropoulos A et al. (2019) *Reuters Institute Digital News Report 2019.* Oxford: Reuters Institute for the Study of Journalism.

Newman N, Fletcher R, Schulz A et al. (2020) *Reuters Institute Digital News Report 2020.* Oxford: Reuters Institute for the Study of Journalism.

Nielsen RK and Graves L (2017) *'News You Don't Believe': Audience Perspectives on Fake News*. Oxford: Reuters Institute for the Study of Journalism.

Nyhan B and Reifler J (2015) Does correcting myths about the flu vaccine work? An experimental evaluation of the effects of corrective information. *Vaccine* 33(3): 459–464. DOI: 10.1016/j.vaccine.2014.11.017.

Pariser E (2012) *The Filter Bubble: What the Internet is Hiding from You*. London: Penguin Books.

Paschen J (2019) Investigating the emotional appeal of fake news using artificial intelligence and human contributions. *Journal of Product & Brand Management* 29(2): 223–233. DOI: 10.1108/JPBM-12-2018-2179.

Pennycook G and Rand DG (2019) Lazy, not biased: Susceptibility to partisan fake news is better explained by lack of reasoning than by motivated reasoning. *Cognition* 188: 39–50. DOI: 10.1016/j.cognition.2018.06.011.

Pennycook G, Cannon TD and Rand DG (2018) Prior exposure increases perceived accuracy of fake news. *Journal of Experimental Psychology: General* 147(12): 1865–1880. DOI: 10.1037/xge0000465.

Perrin A and Anderson M (2019) Share of U.S. adults using social media, including Facebook, is mostly unchanged since 2018. *Pew Research Centre*, 10 April. Available at: www.pewresearch.org/fact-tank/2019/04/10/share-of-u-s-adults-using-social-media-including-facebook-is-mostly-unchanged-since-2018/.

Royal Society for Public Health (2019) *Moving the Needle: Promoting Vaccination Uptake Across the Life Course*. London: Royal Society for Public Health.

Schröder KC (2015) News media old and new: Fluctuating audiences, news repertoires and locations of consumption. *Journalism Studies* 16(1): 60–78. DOI: 10.1080/1461670X.2014.890332.

Silverman C (2016) This analysis shows how viral fake election news stories outperformed real news on Facebook. *Buzzfeed*, 16 November. Available at: www.buzzfeednews.com/article/craigsilverman/viral-fake-election-news-outperformed-real-news-on-facebook#.qpj6qJ1MP.

Smith TC (2017) Vaccine rejection and hesitancy: A review and call to action. *Open Forum Infectious Diseases* 4(3). DOI: 10.1093/ofid/ofx146.

Stecula DA, Kuru O and Hall Jamieson K (2020) How trust in experts and media use affect acceptance of common anti-vaccination claims. *Harvard Kennedy School Misinformation Review*. DOI: 10.37016/mr-2020-007.

Sunstein CR (2011) *Going to Extremes: How Like Minds Unite and Divide*. Oxford: Oxford University Press.

Tangherlini TR, Roychowdhury V, Glenn B et al. (2016) 'Mommy blogs' and the vaccination exemption narrative: Results from a machine-learning approach for story aggregation on parenting social media sites. *JMIR Public Health and Surveillance* 2(2): e166. DOI: 10.2196/publichealth.6586.

Timm KMF, Maibach EW, Boykoff M et al. (2020) The prevalence and rationale for presenting an opposing viewpoint in climate change reporting: Findings from a U.S. national survey of TV weathercasters. *Weather, Climate, and Society* 12(1): 103–115. DOI: 10.1175/WCAS-D-19-0063.1.

Torabi Asr F and Taboada M (2019) Big Data and quality data for fake news and misinformation detection. *Big Data & Society* 6(1). DOI: 10.1177/2053951719843310.

Tsang SJ (2020) Issue stance and perceived journalistic motives explain divergent audience perceptions of fake news. *Journalism*. DOI: 10.1177/1464884920926002.

Vosoughi S, Roy D and Aral S (2018) The spread of true and false news online. *Science* 359(6380): 1146–1151. DOI: 10.1126/science.aap9559.

Wagner MC and Boczkowski PJ (2019) The reception of fake news: The interpretations and practices that shape the consumption of perceived misinformation. *Digital Journalism* 7(7): 870–885. DOI: 10.1080/21670811.2019.1653208.

Wardle C (2018) Lessons for reporting in an age of disinformation. *First Draft News*, 27 December. Available at: https://firstdraftnews.org/latest/5-lessons-for-reporting-in-an-age-of-disinformation/.

Wardle C and Derakhshan H (2017) *Information Disorder: Toward an Interdisciplinary Framework for Research and Policy Making*. DGI(2017)09. Brussels: Council of Europe.

Washington HA (2006) *Medical Apartheid: The Dark History of Medical Experimentation on Black Americans from Colonial Times to the Present*. First edition. New York: Doubleday.

Weeks BE (2015) Emotions, partisanship, and misperceptions: How anger and anxiety moderate the effect of partisan bias on susceptibility to political misinformation: Emotions and misperceptions. *Journal of Communication* 65(4): 699–719. DOI: 10.1111/jcom.12164.

Weng L, Flammini A, Vespignani A et al. (2013) Competition among memes in a world with limited attention. *Scientific Reports* 3(1): 2304. DOI: 10.1038/srep02304.

Wineburg S, McGrew S, Breakstone J et al. (2016) *Evaluating Information: The Cornerstone of Civic Online Reasoning*. Stanford: Stanford History Education Group.

Wood T and Porter E (2019) The elusive backfire effect: Mass attitudes' steadfast factual adherence. *Political Behavior* 41(1): 135–163. DOI: 10.1007/s11109-018-9443-y.

World Health Organisation (2019) Ten threats to global health in 2019. In: *World Health Organisation*. Available at: www.who.int/news-room/feature-stories/ten-threats-to-global-health-in-2019.

Wu T (2017) Blind spot: The attention economy and the law. *Antitrust Law Journal* 82: 771–806.

5   Countermeasures

Developing effective countermeasures for online disinformation is an urgent goal, but it is also a challenging one that presents conceptual, practical, and regulatory difficulties. Conceptual difficulties arise because definitions of the problem vary considerably and the boundaries between disinformation, opinion, and other kinds of problem content such as hate speech are often unclear. Practical issues stem from the huge volume of content that flows through online platforms, which makes it difficult to develop and apply fair and consistent principles for moderation. At the same time, from a regulatory perspective, there are significant concerns about the legal, ethical, and democratic implications of restricting free expression and granting platforms an (unaccountable) power to determine what is acceptable. So while there is broad agreement that disinformation countermeasures are necessary, there is far less clarity about what can and should be done.

Each of the above challenges is compounded by major gaps in our understanding of online disinformation. Research on countermeasures is in its infancy and tends to be concentrated on the Global North. More fundamentally, the platforms have largely declined to share relevant data with independent researchers, which greatly impedes efforts to assess the scale and nature of the problem and to evaluate the effectiveness of interventions. This is the glaring anomaly at the heart of disinformation countermeasures: the platforms have data that could illuminate the problem and its mitigation, but, to date, this has not been made available.

An important context for these debates is the shift in policymakers' stance towards the platforms. A culture of deference has given way to greater demands for action and accountability. Concerns about disinformation are only one component of this shift. In Europe, policymakers have pressured the platforms to act on illegal content and data protection among other issues. In the process, the case for regulating the platforms has gathered steady momentum. For their part, the platforms' response to disinformation has been sporadic and opaque. Each platform has pursued its own policies and there is minimal oversight to ascertain whether those policies are effective or fair (Gillespie 2018; Gorwa et al. 2020).

On some issues, the platforms have developed opposing policies. Ahead of the 2020 US presidential election, Twitter announced a blanket ban on political advertising while Facebook remained steadfast in its refusal to fact-check political ads (Ortutay and Anderson 2020). This position has come under intense pressure in the wake of the Covid-19 crisis and the Black Lives Matter protests. As the platforms are increasingly pressured to do something, the big question is whether their responses will be informed by evidence and open to scrutiny.

The aim of this chapter is not to assess each and every intervention, but to highlight the key developments and debates shaping disinformation countermeasures. We suggest these measures can be broadly divided into three areas: technological approaches, audience-focused approaches, and legal and regulatory approaches. These countermeasures are proposed and developed by a wide range of stakeholders including the platforms, policymakers, independent researchers, NGOs, and actors across the media industry. In reviewing these countermeasures, it is clear that there are no quick fixes for online disinformation and no single approach will be sufficient. More immediate actions, such as fact-checking and content removals, need to be complemented with long-term strategies to regulate online communication, upskill audiences, and safeguard independent journalism. As a case study, we review the EU's response to disinformation as a multi-pronged approach that targets such long-term and short-term objectives. Throughout the chapter, we emphasise the importance of robust research and oversight to ensure that countermeasures do not cause further harm through unintended consequences.

Technological approaches

In response to external pressures, the platforms increasingly rely on technological or algorithmic solutions to moderate the large volumes of content that are uploaded to their systems. At the same time, many policymakers, start-ups, and independent researchers also advocate technological solutions to detect disinformation and 'inauthentic' behaviour (see EPRS 2019). The chief advantage of a technological approach is the promise of moderating content at speed and scale. The platforms already rely on algorithmic moderation to detect illegal content including hate speech, child pornography, copyright infringements, and terrorist propaganda. Developments here have been driven in part by regulatory measures such as the EU Code of Conduct on Countering Illegal Hate Speech Online (2016) and Germany's Network Enforcement Act (NetzDG 2017), which require platforms to take down illegal content within 24 hours. Yet, while algorithmic moderation offers advantages in speed and scale, there are also major shortcomings in terms of accuracy, reliability, and oversight.

In essence, technological countermeasures rely on machine learning and neural network models to automate the process of content moderation (see Gorwa et al. 2020). Although specific techniques vary considerably, the overall aim is to classify content into problem categories (e.g. clickbait, fake news) or to match uploads against a database of problem content (e.g. known cases of disinformation). The development of large-scale databases for matching content is primarily the preserve of the major platforms. For example, through the self-regulatory Global Internet Forum to Counter Terrorism (GIFCT), Google, Facebook, Twitter, and Microsoft maintain a database of terrorist content. However, there is little transparency and accountability regarding how content is entered into the database, how much content is flagged incorrectly, or how many appeals are issued and upheld (Gorwa et al. 2020).

Classification algorithms are developed by both the platforms and independent researchers. Of course, the latter are disadvantaged by their dependence on publicly available data and the limited API access offered by some platforms (see Freelon 2018). Moreover, the platforms' algorithms remain secret while independent researchers typically open up their methods to scrutiny. Many independent researchers have developed useful and freely available tools for verification and analysis. To name a few: Botometer® evaluates the likelihood that a given Twitter account is an automated bot; InVid detects manipulations in image and video content; and Hoaxy uses web crawlers to extract links from fake news websites and the corresponding debunks from fact-checking sites.

In broad terms, such algorithms may be understood for their focus on the text, context, or knowledge claims associated with a piece of content. Text-based algorithms examine linguistic and stylistic characteristics such as word use, writing style, grammar, and emotional tone. The algorithms developed by independent researchers are typically trained on datasets of fact-checked content to predict disinformation and on datasets of professional journalism to predict high-quality content (Zhang et al. 2018). Context-based algorithms identify 'inauthentic' patterns in social media behaviour. For example, bot scores are calculated for Twitter accounts by examining irregularities in profile and account behaviour; although these methods are prone to error (Gorwa and Guilbeault 2020). Finally, knowledge-based algorithms interrogate factual claims and can assist human fact-checkers by extracting factual claims and known false claims (see Graves 2018). Whatever the specific technique, technological approaches are locked into an arms race with bad actors. As the latter learn how detection algorithms work, they adapt their tactics accordingly.

Moreover, technological approaches are often highly unreliable. For all the hype about artificial intelligence, it is human intelligence that is required to appreciate nuance and context (see Mühlhoff 2019). Without human intelligence to review algorithmic judgements, there are significant risks of over-zealous and error-prone moderation. This was evident during the Covid-19 crisis when social-distancing measures restricted the availability of human moderators. As a result, in March 2020 the platforms acknowledged that groundless content removals were likely to increase (Stokel-Walker 2020). In the following months, Facebook blamed a 'bug' in its systems for mistakenly marking news stories as spam (Heilweil 2020) while Twitter erroneously flagged tweets containing the words 'oxygen' and 'frequency' as conspiracy theories (Serrano 2020).

Even without the personnel challenges created by Covid-19, there are major concerns about unjustified content removals (Banchik 2020). Human oversight for content moderation is often outsourced to poorly resourced contractors in the Global South (Roberts 2019). Meanwhile, platforms' resources and interventions are heavily biased towards the Global North, leaving millions of people across the world exposed to disinformation and harmful content. In 2018, the UN accused Facebook of playing a 'determining role' in the incitement of genocidal violence against Myanmar's Rohingya population. An investigation by Reuters revealed that Facebook's human moderators and its algorithmic moderation system were unable to comprehend the regions' languages (Stecklow 2018). Although the platforms have conquered global communication, their technological and human resources are currently ill-equipped to accommodate the diversity of world cultures and languages.

The labelled datasets used by independent researchers also have major constraints. As Mühlhoff (2019: 2) argues, the scarce resource in AI projects 'is neither algorithms nor computing power but rather the availability of training and verification data, which is ultimately obtained through human participation'. Currently, there is a deep reliance on journalists and fact-checkers to annotate training data, which has resulted in datasets that are either small or limited in scope (Torabi

Asr and Taboada 2019). Moreover, as these small datasets are biased towards the topics that primarily interest journalists and fact-checkers (i.e. politics), there is a danger that detection tools will be ineffective for large amounts of disinformation.

Nevertheless, the possibility of detecting problem content at speed and scale remains the major advantage of technological approaches. It is also true that the accuracy and reliability of detection algorithms are likely to improve over time. However, algorithmic moderation requires close scrutiny and it is important that all stakeholders – and most especially policymakers – understand the limitations, the potential for bias, and the required levels of oversight.

Audience-focused approaches

In tandem with efforts to curb the visibility of disinformation, audience-focused approaches aim to equip citizens with the necessary information and skills to evaluate content for themselves. As outlined below, efforts here are concentrated on advancing research into the effectiveness of providing information corrections and 'inoculations' as well as the expansion of fact-checking and media literacy initiatives.

Research insights: There is growing evidence that providing succinct and repeated corrections can counter disinformation (Lewandowsky et al. 2012, 2017). However, further research is needed to better understand the circumstances that support successful correction. In particular, longitudinal studies are needed to understand whether the effects are long-lasting. In their meta-analysis of current research, Walter and Tukachinsky (2020) found that corrections are less effective when the disinformation was originally attributed to a credible source, when people have been exposed to the disinformation multiple times prior to correction, and when there is a time delay between the initial exposure and the correction. Other studies indicate that corrections may reduce false perceptions but do little to challenge underlying attitudes. For example, in the context of politics, Nyhan et al. (2019) found that corrections can reduce misperceptions, but often have a minimal effect on political preferences.

As an alternative to corrections, research on inoculation or 'prebunking' finds that the effects of disinformation can be neutralised by warning people about the threat of disinformation and explaining how manipulation tactics work (Cook et al. 2017; Roozenbeek et al. 2020; van der Linden et al. 2017). The underlying expectation is that inoculation provides people with a counter-argument to reject disinformation when they encounter it. For example, Roozenbeek et al.

(2020) found that exposure to a game-based intervention improved participants' latent ability to identify manipulation tactics when they subsequently encountered disinformation. Relatedly, another promising strand of research finds that simply prompting people to think about the accuracy of a message greatly improves their ability to reject disinformation while also reducing the intention to share disinformation (Fazio 2020; Pennycook et al. 2020). To move beyond experimental settings, some researchers are investigating how to integrate the above research findings into fact-checking and media literacy practices (Tully et al. 2020; Vraga et al. 2020).

Yet, while researchers and practitioners are developing a consensus around best-practice, the platforms remain free to determine their own courses of action. During Covid-19, those who interacted with disinformation on Facebook received only generic messages and links to the World Health Organisation (WHO); there was no indication of what content instigated the message and so no refutation of specific false claims. The cornerstone of the platforms' response to Covid-19 was the promotion of links to authoritative sources including the WHO and, to a lesser extent, fact-checking organisations.

Fact checking: Fact-checking is a specific type of correction that has grown considerably in recent years. In the early 2000s, fact-checking was largely confined to non-profit organisations in the US. Fact-checking has grown internationally through funding and support from governments and the platforms. A recent Poynter review noted a transition towards a for-profit business model with Facebook's Third Party Fact-Checking Program as the main source of income for many fact-checking organisations (Mantas 2020). Although support for fact-checking has increased considerably, research on its effectiveness is mixed. Public engagement with fact-checks appears to be highly selective. People tend to endorse fact-checks that support their views and avoid those that are incongruent (Hameleers and van der Meer 2020). There is also some dispute about consistency and reliability as fact-checking organisations vary in their structures, methods, and dissemination strategies. To formalise standards, the International Fact-Checking Network (IFCN) was launched by the Poynter Institute in September 2015 and it now plays an institutionally dominant role in the world of fact-checking. Facebook, for example, will only partner with organisations that have been certified by the IFCN.

Many fact-checking organisations focus specifically on claims made by politicians while some digital outlets, such as Snopes, cover a wider range of online claims. In either case, certain topics and claims are more amenable to fact checking than others (Graves 2016). Consider, for example, claims about the relationship between immigration and crime. Far-right extremists frequently cite crime statistics to attack immigrants, but determining the correct way to interpret crime statistics is not straightforward. In fact, it is the subject of ongoing academic dispute (see Ousey and Kubrin 2018). In contrast, there is a clear scientific consensus for topics such as climate change and the safety of the MMR vaccine, which makes it easier to establish the facts and to refute false claims. As fact-checking is limited in terms of audience reach, Graves (2016) argues that fact-checks are better understood as a public resource. In other words, a particular fact-check might not have a direct impact on the audiences who were exposed to disinformation, but it can provide additional ammunition for those who are working to counter disinformation on that issue.

Media and information literacy: As with fact-checking, there has been a notable increase in support for media and information literacy initiatives. Many countries have provided additional funding for media literacy programmes (see Funke and Flamini 2020). Campaigns and educational programmes are supported by an array of stakeholders including educators, policymakers, librarians, and the platforms. For example, Google funded the Poynter Institute's MediaWise project, which is aimed at teenagers while the company updated its digital safety programme for children to include a media literacy component.

Overall, media and information literacy approaches suffer somewhat from a lack of conceptual coherence. Since 2007, UNESCO has championed 'media and information literacy' as an umbrella concept that incorporates competencies relating to media, information, and digital technologies. However, media literacy and information literacy developed as distinct fields and are often treated as such by researchers and practitioners. Media literacy education rests on the reasonable assumption that developing analytical skills and knowledge about media structures should help people make more informed judgements about the content they consume. The kind of knowledge emphasised by media literacy reflects its origins in the mass media era; it encourages reflection on issues of media ownership, production practices, and representation (Potter 2020). In contrast, digital and information literacy developed in response to online communication technologies. Here, the emphasis is on competencies for finding and evaluating information. To complicate matters, new subfields are emerging such as news literacy, data literacy, and digital literacy.

In fact, literacy education is increasingly viewed as a panacea for a wide-range of problems. There are regular calls for the promotion of environmental literacy, scientific literacy, and emotional literacy among others. Although the intentions are benign, there is clearly a danger of overloading education with literacy programmes. Moreover, most issues cut across multiple literacy competencies. For example, online disinformation about climate change could be addressed through scientific literacy and environmental literacy as much as media and information literacy. Another challenge is that media and information literacy is typically targeted at the young and delivered through educational programmes. Yet, older adults are more likely to struggle with online disinformation and with digital technologies more generally (Guess et al. 2020). Without addressing the lifelong literacy needs of older age-groups, there is a real risk of allowing a generation gap to widen.

Finally, as with almost all of the countermeasures discussed in this chapter, the effectiveness of media and information literacy is not clear. Some studies find that exposure to media literacy education predicts resilience to political disinformation (Kahne and Bowyer 2017), but other studies caution that media literacy endows individuals with a false sense of confidence (Bulger and Davison 2018). More fundamentally, as danah boyd (2018) argues, encouraging people to adopt a critical stance towards online information isn't necessarily helpful. After all, bad actors already employ the rhetoric of critical thinking to 'ask questions' about the legitimacy of the news media and scientific evidence.

Treated in isolation, a weakness of all the audience-focused countermeasures discussed above is that they place emphasis on the individual's responsibility to develop and apply new skills (Bulger and Davidson 2018). However, few argue that audience-focused countermeasures are sufficient in themselves. Rather, they are just one component of the wider effort to stabilise the information environment. Moreover, technological and audience-focused approaches can be combined to change the dynamics of social sharing. Twitter is currently testing a new feature that prompts people to read an article before sharing it. Adding elements of friction – whether combined with content labelling and media literacy prompts or not – may go some way to breaking the cycle of instantaneous reaction.

Legal and regulatory approaches

From a legal and regulatory perspective, online disinformation operates in a grey area. Although it may cause significant public harm, it is not illegal in most democratic countries. Meanwhile, regulatory structures for online content were designed for a different era. The rules that exempt platforms from liability for the content they host were designed decades ago to encourage the growth of online businesses and services.

Similarly, regulatory structures for media were designed for a pre-internet world in which there were relatively clear boundaries between media production, distribution, and consumption. There has been an urgent need to update these legal and regulatory structures for many years irrespective of current concerns about disinformation and related problem content.

In recent years, some countries have created new categories of speech such as 'disinformation' or 'legal but harmful content' (Funke and Flamini 2020), but the implementation of new regulations is not without controversy. For democratic governments, policies that aim to counter disinformation should also respect freedom of thought and freedom of expression. For authoritarian governments and democratic states that are 'backsliding' into authoritarianism, concerns about online disinformation are an opportunity to exercise more control over the media landscape, political opponents, and citizens. For example, Malaysia's Anti-Fake News Act was introduced prior to national elections and aided the censorship of government critics including investigative journalists (Yeung 2018). Although the law was repealed in 2019 by the reform government, similar laws have been passed across Southeast Asia and East Africa, which enable authorities to impose severe penalties for the publication or distribution of disinformation (Sasipornkarn 2019). In authoritarian contexts, there is often little regard for distinctions between critical opinions and false information or between the intentional creation of disinformation and unintentional engagement with it. Brazil's recent law is perhaps the most severe in this regard as it criminalises membership of online groups that share disinformation where disinformation is loosely defined as content that poses a risk to 'social peace or to the economic order' (Tiwari and Ben-Avie 2020). The law also erodes online anonymity as social media users are expected to provide valid identity documents.

In many countries, laws against 'fake news' are accompanied by internet shutdowns. Shutdowns have become commonplace in Africa and Asia and are often justified on the pretext of countering disinformation (Taye 2019). For example, the Sri Lankan government blocked access to social media platforms to avoid unverified reports and speculation in the wake of the 2019 terror attacks (Ellis-Petersen 2019). These and similar bills are widely criticised for their potentially chilling impact on media freedom and, in particular, investigative journalism. However, it is important to note that anti-terrorism legislation in democratic states can have a similar impact. The UK's 2019 'counter-terrorism and border security' bill, which criminalises the expression of 'reckless opinions and beliefs', has been controversial for its potential misuse and, in particular, the potential threat to investigative journalism (Index on Censorship 2019).

While authoritarian governments seek to punish those who create and share disinformation, democratic governments tend to place greater emphasis on the platforms' responsibility. In most jurisdictions, the removal of illegal content works through a 'notice and take down' procedure. Platforms must remove illegal content when they are alerted to it, but there is no onus to actively seek it out and platforms are not liable for the content created by their users. This concept of liability is central to the development of the internet as we know it today. For Kosseff (2019), the 1996 US Communication Act is 'the law that created the Internet' because it allows content to move freely across the Internet without liability. New platforms were then free to develop their own moderation policies or 'community standards' for content. Meanwhile, internet governance was restricted to a select group of (US dominated) organisations overseeing technical standards and infrastructure issues such as domain names. In the early 1990s few could have anticipated how online technologies would evolve and self-regulation without liability appeared to be a natural framework for a decentralised, global communication system. That framework is no longer fit for purpose as a small group of companies now dominate digital commerce and communication (see Chapter 3). The idea of setting supervisory standards for major platforms is increasingly to the fore. In France and the UK, there are proposals to create central authorities for social networks to address a range of issues including disinformation and the EU's proposed Digital Services Act is expected to revise platform liability.

To date, policymakers have primarily perceived disinformation in terms of foreign meddling in democratic elections. The establishment of task forces and parliamentary committees on foreign interference appears to have been the predominant international response to claims about a Russian influence campaign during the 2016 US presidential election (Funke and Flamini 2020). However, it is increasingly clear that domestic actors, including political parties, are a major source of disinformation. In either case, the microtargeting of voters has been identified as a key mechanism for disinformation. One option is to limit microtargeting categories and especially in relation to personal categories. For example, the EU's landmark General Data Protection Regulation (GDPR) considers some topics – including political ideology, sexuality, and health status – to be sensitive categories of personal data, which require special treatment. Platforms could also be required to make microtargeting transparent by providing information about adverts including the size of the targeted audience, the criteria for selecting recipients, and the source of payment. In the EU, the platforms have already committed to providing this information for political advertising, but their public archives have been heavily criticised for inconsistencies and errors (ERGA 2020). In the US, the Honest Ads Act was originally proposed in 2017 with bipartisan support. It proposes to impose broadcast disclosure rules on platform advertising and would require platforms to verify who is funding political ads.

Clearly, the regulatory environment has failed to keep pace with the rapid evolution of digital platforms. The crux of the challenge is to develop regulatory structures that are effective at scale while maintaining fundamental freedoms. To date, US platforms have dominated the global internet, but there is no reason to suppose that the influential platforms of the future will be based in countries that champion freedom of expression, if even only in principle. The past 20 years of the web have shown that platforms can wane in popularity, which means that any regulation needs to be mindful of future change.

Case study: the EU response

Here we review the EU-wide response to disinformation, but it is important to note that EU member states are free to determine their own approach. Thus far, the response of individual states has varied greatly (Council of the European Union 2019). For example, the Baltic states have devised their own disinformation strategies with a specific focus on countering Russian disinformation while France and Germany have passed laws allowing courts to issue take-down orders for fake accounts. Amid the Covid-19 crisis, Hungary adopted emergency measures permitting prison terms for those accused of spreading disinformation about the government response. This follows years of regressive actions against media freedom in Hungary and its neighbouring states (Repucci 2019). Although such restrictions are antithetical to the EU's professed values, there has been little by way of sanctions or repercussions. As such, the EU's ambitious plan to counter disinformation faces internal as well as external obstacles.

Disinformation is not illegal under EU law or under the laws of most member states, but it is recognised as a potential threat to democracy and to the health and security of EU citizens (European Commission 2018a). In many respects, the EU's evolving position on disinformation may be understood as a reaction to a series of crises: from the Russian-Ukrainian conflict through fears of election interference to Covid-19. However, there is also a clear recognition that disinformation is symptomatic of wider societal issues including 'economic insecurity, rising extremism, and cultural shifts [that] generate anxiety and provide a breeding ground for disinformation campaigns to foster societal tensions, polarisation, and distrust' (European Commission 2018a: 4). To address this, the current European Commission, which will serve until 2024, has outlined three priorities: strengthening media freedom, making platforms more accountable, and protecting the democratic process (Stolton and Makszimov 2020).

A major component of this is the Digital Services Act, which is expected to be unveiled in 2021. It is widely anticipated that this legislative package will set out clear rules for platform liability, introduce oversight for algorithmic content moderation, and sanctions for non-compliance. In regards to disinformation on online platforms, it will mark a significant shift from a self-regulatory framework towards a co-regulatory one. The self-regulatory approach was adopted in the EU's 2018 Action Plan against Disinformation (European Commission 2018b). This plan aimed to reinforce EU-wide capabilities in four key areas: improving disinformation detection; coordinating responses by member states; cooperating with platforms; and empowering EU citizens. There is insufficient scope to discuss all the components of the EU response, which includes funding for research, fact-checking and media literacy initiatives. In 2020, the European Digital Media Observatory was established to consolidate these activities and to direct the work of disinformation research hubs across Europe. Here, we focus on the weaknesses of the self-regulatory approach, direct actions against Russian disinformation, and the wider regulatory actions that are transforming how the internet is governed in the EU.

Ahead of the 2019 European Parliament elections, the EU established a self-regulatory and voluntary Code of Practice for the platforms and online advertisers (European Commission 2018c). Signatories – including Facebook, Google, and Twitter – were obliged to take measures to disrupt advertising revenues for disinformation, address the prevalence of fake accounts and bots, and make political advertising more transparent. To address the latter, the platforms established publicly accessible archives for political advertising. However, compliance reports criticised the platforms' ambiguous definitions of political advertising and found their archives to be underdeveloped, incomplete, and bug-ridden (ERGA 2020).

A subsequent review by the European Commission (2020a) concluded that self-regulation should be replaced with co-regulation along with sanctions and redress mechanisms to ensure compliance with the rules. These criticisms intensified during the Covid-19 crisis as the EU called on the platforms to cooperate with researchers and fact checkers and to provide more transparency for citizens who have engaged with disinformation on their platforms (European Commission 2020b). The newly created European Digital Media Observatory is expected to play a lead role in organising data access for fact-checkers and researchers in order to monitor disinformation trends across Europe.

In parallel, the EU has adopted a more confrontational approach to countering Russian disinformation. The East StratCom Task Force was established in 2015 to monitor and analyse Russian disinformation. Embedded within the EU's diplomatic service, East StratCom publishes a weekly Disinformation Review outlining examples of 'pro-Kremlin disinformation' while its website – www.EUvsDisinfo.eu – provides a database of debunked disinformation. In 2017, two additional Task Forces were established to counter anti-EU narratives in the Western Balkans and in the Middle East and North Africa. East StratCom's abrasive messaging has drawn frequent criticism. In 2018, it was required to amend its database when three Dutch media outlets launched a legal action over their designation as disinformation actors. In 2020, researchers at the University of Manchester accused East StratCom of misrepresenting Russian media articles by omitting contextual details to distort the nature of the original content. The researchers concluded that 'East StratCom is jeopardising [the EU's] credibility as an evidence-driven policymaker [and] giving valuable ammunition to Russian state media' (Hutchings and Tolz 2020).

More generally, the EU's response to disinformation is tied to wider regulatory developments. In recent years, the EU has challenged the dominance of US platforms by calling for a 'balanced regulatory framework' that would support the 'emergence of new online platforms in Europe' (European Commission 2016: 4). Recent regulations – including the General Data Protection Regulation (GDPR), the controversial Copyright Directive, and the Audiovisual Media Services Directive (AVMSD) – have all set parameters for how online companies operate within the EU.

Regulations in Europe and elsewhere have raised concerns about the global internet 'splintering' across regional borders. However, it may also be argued that the current problem stems from the existence of corporations with global reach and an absence of corresponding governance mechanisms. One benefit of the EU's approach to disinformation is that it is reshaping governance models to include key stakeholders such as public authorities, the platforms, media organisations, fact-checkers, researchers, and civil society.

Conclusion

In many respects, current efforts to counteract online disinformation appear to be piecemeal and uncoordinated. However, these are early days and a deeper understanding of the problem – including its wide-ranging and overlapping causes – needs to be developed. The implications of proposed countermeasures, including the potential for unintended consequences, also needs close scrutiny. Some of these issues have been touched upon in this chapter, but there are many other ethical, social, and political implications. To take one example, Twitter's blanket ban on political advertising may negatively impact democratic politics as it favours established candidates while disadvantaging political newcomers (McGregor 2019). Thus, while calls for action on disinformation are understandable, action for the sake of it – or for the sake of PR – will not address the underlying issues.

The countermeasures put in place by all actors must be based on evidence and open to external scrutiny. This means that access to the platform's data is a prerequisite for developing effective countermeasures. Currently, independent researchers and policymakers are unable to determine the true scale and impact of online disinformation. At the same time, it is clear that countering disinformation is difficult. Measures that detect and counteract individual cases of disinformation are important, but they do not address the underlying societal dynamics that make disinformation appealing in the first place. As outlined in Chapter 3, disinformation narratives can be difficult to counteract because they are cognitively and emotionally appealing for some segments of the audiences. In other words, we suggest that countering disinformation rests on a deeper transformation of the digital environment; one in which transparency and oversight are built-in to communication structures. In the next chapter we argue that efforts to combat disinformation need to be considered in broader terms of strengthening democratic communication, participation, and trust.

References

Banchik AV (2020) Disappearing acts: Content moderation and emergent practices to preserve at-risk human rights–related content. *New Media & Society*. DOI: 10.1177/1461444820912724.

boyd d (2018) You think you want media literacy... do you? In: *Data & Society*. Available at: https://points.datasociety.net/you-think-you-want-media-literacy-do-you-7cad6af18ec2.

Bulger M and Davison P (2018) The promises, challenges and futures of media literacy. *Journal of Media Literacy Education* 10(1): 1–21.

Clayton K, Blair S, Busam JA et al. (2019) Real solutions for fake news? Measuring the effectiveness of general warnings and fact-check tags in reducing belief in false stories on social media. *Political Behavior*. DOI: 10.1007/s11109-019-09533-0.

Cook J, Lewandowsky S and Ecker UKH (2017) Neutralizing misinformation through inoculation: Exposing misleading argumentation techniques reduces their influence. Manalo E (ed.) *PLOS ONE* 12(5): e0175799. DOI: 10.1371/journal.pone.0175799.

Council of the European Union (2019) *Report of the Presidency to the European Council on 20–21 June 2019, on countering disinformation and the lessons learnt from the European elections*. Brussels: Council of the European Union. Available at: www.romania2019.eu/wp-content/uploads/2017/11/raport-consiliu.pdf.

Craft S, Ashley S and Maksl A (2017) News media literacy and conspiracy theory endorsement. *Communication and the Public* 2(4): 388–401. DOI: 10.1177/2057047317725539.

East StratCom Task Force (2018) *Questions and Answers about the East StratCom Task Force*. 12 May. Brussels: East StratCom Task Force. Available at: https://eeas.europa.eu/headquarters/headquarters-homepage_en/2116/%20Questions%20and%20Answers%20about%20the%20East%20StratCom%20Task%20Force.

Ellis-Petersen H (2019) Social media shut down in Sri Lanka in bid to stem misinformation. *The Guardian*, 21 April. Available at: www.theguardian.com/world/2019/apr/21/social-media-shut-down-in-sri-lanka-in-bid-to-stem-misinformation.

EPRS (2019) *Automated Tackling of Disinformation*. European Parliamentary Research Service.

ERGA (2020) *ERGA Report on Disinformation: Assessment of the Implementation of the Code of Practice*. Brussels: European Regulators Group for Audiovisual Media Services (ERGA).

European Commission (2016) *Communication on Online Platforms and the Digital Single Market*. Brussels: European Commission.

European Commission (2018a) *Tackling Online Disinformation: A European Approach.* COM(2018) 236, 26 April. Brussels: European Commission.

European Commission (2018b) *Action Plan against Disinformation.* Brussels: European Commission. Available at: https://ec.europa.eu/commission/sites/beta-political/files/eu-communication-disinformation-euco-05122018_en.pdf.

European Commission (2018c) *EU Code of Practice on Disinformation.* 26 September. Brussels: European Commission. Available at: https://ec.europa.eu/newsroom/dae/document.cfm?doc_id=54454.

European Commission (2020a) *Assessment of the Implementation of the Code of Practice on Disinformation.* 8 May. Luxembourg: European Commission.

European Commission (2020b) *Communication: The EU's Fight Against Covid-19 Disinformation.* 10 June. Brussels: European Commission.

Fazio L (2020) Pausing to consider why a headline is true or false can help reduce the sharing of false news. *Harvard Kennedy School Misinformation Review.* DOI: 10.37016/mr-2020-009.

Freelon D (2018) Computational Research in the Post-API Age. *Political Communication* 35(4): 665–668. DOI: 10.1080/10584609.2018.1477506.

Funke D and Flamini D (2020) A guide to anti-misinformation actions around the world. *Poynter*, updated. Available at: www.poynter.org/ifcn/anti-misinformation-actions/.

Gillespie T (2018) *Custodians of the Internet: Platforms, Content Moderation, and the Hidden Decisions That Shape Social Media.* New Haven: Yale University Press.

Gorwa R and Guilbeault D (2020) Unpacking the social media bot: A typology to guide research and policy. *Policy & Internet* 12(2): 225–248. DOI: 10.1002/poi3.184.

Gorwa R, Binns R and Katzenbach C (2020) Algorithmic content moderation: Technical and political challenges in the automation of platform governance. *Big Data & Society* 7(1). DOI: 10.1177/2053951719897945.

Graves L (2016) *Deciding What's True: The Rise of Political Fact-Checking in American Journalism.* New York: Columbia University Press.

Graves L (2018) *Understanding the Promise and Limits of Automated Fact-Checking.* Oxford: Reuters Institute for the Study of Journalism. Available at: https://reutersinstitute.politics.ox.ac.uk/sites/default/files/2018-02/graves_factsheet_180226%20FINAL.pdf.

Guess AM, Nyhan B and Reifler J (2020) Exposure to untrustworthy websites in the 2016 US election. *Nature Human Behaviour* 4(5): 472–480. DOI: 10.1038/s41562-020-0833-x.

Hameleers M and van der Meer TGLA (2020) Misinformation and polarization in a high-choice media environment: How effective are political fact-checkers? *Communication Research* 47(2): 227–250. DOI: 10.1177/0093650218819671.

Heilweil R (2020) Facebook is flagging some coronavirus news posts as spam. *Vox*, 17 March. Available at: www.vox.com/recode/2020/3/17/21183557/coronavirus-youtube-facebook-twitter-social-media.

Hutchings S and Tolz V (2020) Covid-19 disinformation: Two short reports on the Russian dimension. In: *Reframing Russia*. Available at: https://reframingrussia.com/2020/04/06/covid-19-disinformation-two-short-reports-on-the-russian-dimension/.

Index on Censorship (n.d.) *Freedom of Expression and the Counter-Terrorism and Border Security Act*. London: Index on Censorship. Available at: www.indexoncensorship.org/2019/02/freedom-of-expression-and-the-counter-terrorism-and-border-security-act/.

Kahne J and Bowyer B (2017) Educating for democracy in a partisan age: Confronting the challenges of motivated reasoning and misinformation. *American Educational Research Journal* 54(1): 3–34. DOI: 10.3102/0002831216679817.

Kosseff J (2019) *The Twenty-Six Words That Created the Internet*. Ithaca: Cornell University Press.

Lewandowsky S, Ecker UKH, Seifert CM et al. (2012) Misinformation and its correction: continued influence and successful debiasing. *Psychological Science in the Public Interest* 13(3): 106–131. DOI: 10.1177/1529100612451018.

Lewandowsky S, Ecker UKH and Cook J (2017) Beyond misinformation: Understanding and coping with the 'post-truth' era. *Journal of Applied Research in Memory and Cognition* 6(4): 353–369. DOI: 10.1016/j.jarmac.2017.07.008.

Mantas H (2020) With the help of platforms, grants and donations, more fact-checking organizations are now for-profit. *Poynter*, 22 June. Available at: www.poynter.org/fact-checking/2020/with-the-help-of-platforms-grants-and-donations-more-fact-checking-organizations-are-now-for-profit/.

McGregor SC (2019) Why Twitter's ban on political ads isn't as good as it sounds. *The Guardian*, 4 November. Available at: www.theguardian.com/commentisfree/2019/nov/04/twitters-political-ads-ban.

Mühlhoff R (2019) Human-aided artificial intelligence: Or, how to run large computations in human brains? Toward a media sociology of machine learning. *New Media & Society*. DOI: 10.1177/1461444819885334.

Nyhan B, Porter E, Reifler J et al. (2019) Taking fact-checks literally but not seriously? The effects of journalistic fact-checking on factual beliefs and candidate favorability. *Political Behavior*. DOI: 10.1007/s11109-019-09528-x.

Ortutay B and Anderson M (2020) Facebook again refuses to ban political ads, even false ones. *AP News*, 9 January. Available at: https://apnews.com/90e5e81f501346f8779cb2f8b8880d9c.

Ousey GC and Kubrin CE (2018) Immigration and crime: Assessing a contentious issue. *Annual Review of Criminology* 1(1): 63–84. DOI: 10.1146/annurev-criminol-032317-092026.

Pennycook G, McPhetres J, Zhang Y et al. (2020) Fighting Covid-19 misinformation on social media: Experimental evidence for a scalable accuracy nudge intervention. Available at: https://psyarxiv.com/uhbk9/.

Porter E and Wood TJ (2020) Why is Facebook so afraid of checking facts? *Wired*, 14 May. Available at: www.wired.com/story/why-is-facebook-so-afraid-of-checking-facts/.

Potter WJ (2020) *Media Literacy*. Ninth edition. Los Angeles: Sage.

Repucci S (2019) *Freedom and the Media: A Downward Spiral*. Washington, DC: Freedom House.

Roberts ST (2019) *Behind the Screen: Content Moderation in the Shadows of Social Media* . New Haven: Yale University Press.

Roozenbeek J, van der Linden S and Nygren T (2020) Prebunking interventions based on the psychological theory of 'inoculation' can reduce susceptibility to misinformation across cultures. *Harvard Kennedy School Misinformation Review*. DOI: 10.37016//mr-2020-008.

Sasipornkarn E (2019) Southeast Asia 'fake news' laws open the door to digital authoritarianism. *Deutsche Welle*, 16 October. Available at: www.dw.com/en/southeast-asia-fake-news-laws-open-the-door-to-digital-authoritarianism/a-50852994.

Serrano J (2020) Twitter: Sorry for putting Covid-19 misinformation labels on your 'oxygen' tweets. *MSM*, 28 June. Available at: www.msn.com/en-us/news/technology/twitter-sorry-for-putting-covid-19-misinformation-labels-on-your-oxygen-tweets/ar-BB16322V.

Shin J and Thorson K (2017) Partisan selective sharing: the biased diffusion of fact-checking messages on social media: sharing fact-checking messages on social media. *Journal of Communication* 67(2): 233–255. DOI: 10.1111/jcom.12284.

Stecklow S (2018) Why Facebook is losing the war on hate speech in Myanmar. *Reuters*, 15 August. Available at: www.reuters.com/investigates/special-report/myanmar-facebook-hate/.

Stokel-Walker C (2020) As humans go home, Facebook and YouTube face a coronavirus crisis. *Wired*, 20 March. Available at: www.wired.co.uk/article/coronavirus-facts-moderators-facebook-youtube.

Stolton S and Makszimov V (n.d.) Platform regulation 'needed' as part of Democracy Action Plan, Jourová says. *Euractiv*. Brussels. Available at: www.euractiv.com/section/digital/news/platform-regulation-needed-as-part-of-democracy-action-plan-jourova-says/.

Taye B (2019) *Targeted, Cut Off, and Left in The Dark: The #KeepItOn Report on Internet Shutdowns in 2019*. New York: Access Now.

Tiwari U and Ben-Avie J (2020) Mozilla's analysis: Brazil's fake news law harms privacy, security, and free expression. In: *Mozilla*. Available at: https://blog.mozilla.org/netpolicy/2020/06/29/brazils-fake-news-law-harms-privacy-security-and-free-expression/.

Torabi Asr F and Taboada M (2019) Big Data and quality data for fake news and misinformation detection. *Big Data & Society* 6(1). DOI: 10.1177/2053951719843310.

Tully M, Vraga EK and Bode L (2020) Designing and testing news literacy messages for social media. *Mass Communication and Society* 23(1): 22–46. DOI: 10.1080/15205436.2019.1604970.

van der Linden SL, Clarke CE and Maibach EW (2015) Highlighting consensus among medical scientists increases public support for vaccines: evidence from a randomized experiment. *BMC Public Health* 15(1): 1207. DOI: 10.1186/s12889-015-2541-4.

Vraga EK, Bode L and Tully M (2020) Creating news literacy messages to enhance expert corrections of misinformation on Twitter. *Communication Research*. DOI: 10.1177/0093650219898094.

Walter N and Tukachinsky R (2020) A meta-analytic examination of the continued influence of misinformation in the face of correction: how powerful is it, why does it happen, and how to stop it? *Communication Research* 47(2): 155–177. DOI: 10.1177/0093650219854600.

Yeung J (2018) Malaysia repeals controversial fake news law. *CNN*, 17 August. Available at: https://edition.cnn.com/2018/08/17/asia/malaysia-fake-news-law-repeal-intl/index.html.

Zhang AX, Robbins M, Bice E et al. (2018) A structured response to misinformation: defining and annotating credibility indicators in news articles. In: *Companion of The Web Conference 2018 on The Web Conference 2018 – WWW '18*. Lyon: ACM Press, pp. 603–612. DOI: 10.1145/3184558.3188731.

6 Conclusion
Post-truth communication

In this concluding chapter, we take a broader view of the relation-ship between communication and democracy. While disinformation is understandably a cause of concern, it is a mistake to isolate the phe-nomenon from the wider social, political, and media contexts in which it operates. Without this wider perspective, there is a risk of trying to fix the symptoms without addressing the causes. To think through the core issues, we turn to Jurgen Habermas (1962/1991) and his seminal writing on the public sphere.

Habermas (1962/1991) argued that Enlightenment philosophers bequeathed two modes of thinking about the democratic role of com-munication. On the first view, the emphasis is on the dissemination of relevant information because access to relevant information is a pre-requisite for making informed judgements. Consequently, it is necessary to protect public communication from interference by state or financial interests. On the second view, the emphasis is on deliberation among citizens because ideas are tested and gain legitimacy through the process of making arguments and defending those arguments against criticism. Consequently, citizens need opportunities to participate – fairly and equally – in public debate. These ideas have given rise to a conceptual model of a public sphere that operates as 'a neutral zone where access to relevant information affecting the public good is widely available, where discussion is free from domination and where all those participating in public debate do so on an equal basis' (Curran 1996: 82). Of course, this ideal understanding of a public sphere never existed in practice.

Habermas and many others have documented how the mass media of the twentieth century were subject to private interests that managed or manipulated public opinion. To a certain extent, disinformation has always been a feature of public spheres where strategic actors vie for power and influence (Chambers 2020). Undoubtedly, these challenges have become more pronounced in the twenty-first century. As outlined in the preceding chapters, a small group of companies have monopolised online communication in ways that undermine quality journalism and allow disinformation and conspiracy theories to proliferate (Persily 2017; Pickard 2020). Although mass media was clearly prone to sensationalism and bias, it lacked the viral speed and scale of social media. Moreover, mass news media, for all their evident faults, 'were primarily designed to communicate the news and information essential for a well-functioning democracy' (Chambers 2020: 5). In contrast, social media platforms have become a major source of public information and debate, but were never designed to function as a public sphere. Platforms have transformed political campaigning and the media institutions that are supposed to hold politicians accountable, but the platforms have not developed democratic norms or standards (Persily 2017). Of course, the assault on quality journalism extends beyond technology. Across the world, media freedom has deteriorated and the 'trend is most acute in Europe, previously a bastion of well-established freedoms' (Repucci 2019: 2). Following the lead of Donald Trump, populist and authoritarian actors equate journalism with 'fake news', bypass established media, and are supported by highly partisan outlets. Against this background, the US is described as undergoing an 'epistemic crisis' (Benkler et al. 2018) while other democracies are characterised as 'disrupted' public spheres (Bennett and Pfetsch 2018).

Onto this, there is a deeper fear that something more fundamental has happened to public communication. It is now commonplace to assert that we live in a post-truth world in which evidence doesn't matter and 'alternative facts' can triumph. Those diagnosing a post-truth era identify a profound shift in attitudes towards ideas of truth, evidence, and expertise (D'Ancona 2017). The fear is that citizens may care less about the truth and be more accepting of disinformation (Hyvönen 2018). Against this, others contest the post-truth diagnosis as a 'slur' against the public (Finlayson 2019) and a misdirection that conceals a deeper crisis of democratic participation (Farkas and Schou 2019).

As we have argued throughout the book, these nuances matter because false perceptions of the problem can lead to the implementation of ill-conceived remedies. The idea that the public at large doesn't care about truth – or at least cares less than in the past – is a bold claim. After all, international surveys indicate that public concern about online disinformation is high (Newman et al. 2019). Moreover, the vitality of human rights movements around the world 'suggests that truth-seeking remains a rallying cry for those who fight to hold power accountable with facts, information, and conviction' (Waisbord 2018: 1867). Thus, it would seem important to maintain a distinction between claims about the public's relationship to truth and the exhibition of post-truth communication by political actors such as Donald Trump.

In what follows, we assess the relationship between truth and trust in the digital environment to argue that digital media needs to develop norms and standards that would help citizens evaluate who and what to trust. More deeply, however, we suggest that finding ways to reinvigorate public participation in democracy is an essential response to the apparent crisis of trust. To this end, we suggest that innovative models of deliberative democracy may help ameliorate information pathologies while supporting opportunities for understanding and cooperation.

Truth and trust in the digital age

Digital media technologies have raised age-old questions about the creation of knowledge and trust. Taking a long historical view, we can see that these challenges have accompanied all radical communication technologies since the development of writing. Socrates worried that the invention of writing would fundamentally undermine structures of knowledge, but printed text and the book went on to become the canonical emblem of knowledge production (Weinberger 2011). Amid talk of a post-truth crisis instigated by digital technology, it is worth reconsidering some of the competing views on knowledge and digital media that accompanied the advent of the web. After all, the free-exchange of information was fundamental to the development of the web, which was designed to support collaboration among researchers (Berners-Lee 2018).

As online communication became mainstream, many theorists welcomed the democratisation of content production and the participatory culture of information sharing (Benkler 2006; Jenkins 2006; Shirky 2009). In *The Wealth of Networks*, Benkler (2006: 10) argued that digital media created 'a new ecosystem of exchange' whereby information sharing and collaboration became a major modality of production alongside the traditional modalities of corporations, government, and non-profit organisations. At the same time, many worried about the decline of expertise and traditional authorities. The culture critic Andrew Keen (200764–5) feared a 'cult of the amateur' in which 'there are no gatekeepers to filter truth from fiction'. As noted in Chapter 4, the decline of traditional gatekeepers brought additional concerns that citizens would become subject to 'filter bubbles' (Pariser 2012) and self-selecting 'echo-chambers' (Sunstein 2011). These ideas have now coalesced into a panic about post-truth communication and an apparent disregard for facts and evidence.

The democratisation of production clearly changed the values attached to different kinds of content. For Dede (2008: 80), the web gave rise to a 'seismic shift in epistemology' whereby the classical understanding of knowledge production as 'formal, evidence-based argumentation using established methodologies' gave way to a form of knowledge production that combines 'facts with other dimensions of human experience, such as opinions, values, and spiritual beliefs'. Similarly, van Zoonen (2012: 56) proposes the idea of 'i-pistemology' to capture 'a contemporary cultural process in which people from all walks of life have come to suspect the knowledge coming from official institutions and experts, and have replaced it with the truth coming from their own individual experience and opinions'. In this context, the free flow of information from multiple sources places a greater burden on citizens who must determine when to place – and withhold – their trust. Trust is a fundamental aspect of daily life as it is not possible to research every piece of information we encounter online or offline. The crucial issue is about how people decide who to trust and what reference points they have to make those decisions. Yet, the rapid evolution of digital communication has occurred without the development of epistemic norms and standards that would guide people through those decisions. As noted in Chapter 2, platforms – and online communication in general – flatten distinctions between different kinds of content and different kinds of content producer. This makes it easy for bad actors to mimic authority or create the appearance of credibility.

At the same time, distrust of government, politicians, and the media has been escalating for many decades (Hanitzsch et al. 2018; Suiter and Fletcher 2020). In some cases, this distrust is underpinned by political polarisation (Tsfati and Ariely 2014) and authoritarian populism (Kellner 2016). The impacts are circular: in one direction, a negative tone towards politics in news media coverage can lead to an erosion of trust (Hopmann et al. 2015). In the other direction, political actors such as Trump can malign the news industry as 'fake news' and embolden radicals to attack journalists (Wong and Levin 2017). In addition, some politicians and partisan media outlets attack the very idea of factual evidence. Of course, this is an old story and one that Hannah Arendt (1954/2006) summarised as the ability to rewrite history and to transform facts into opinions.

One lens through which to view polarisation and declining trust in news media is the 'hostile media phenomenon' (Vallone et al. 1985) where polarised groups see media coverage as hostile to their own group identity. Perceptions of hostile coverage shape trust in mainstream media outlets (Tsfati and Cohen 2005) and towards policy issues such as climate change (Kim 2011). In the US, low trust in media is associated with polarisation and partisan media consumption. In 2004, Jones found that trust in media was low among conservative Republicans and especially those who listened to political talk radio. Subsequent studies have affirmed this trend, but it should be noted that this is primarily a US phenomenon rather than a universal one (Suiter and Fletcher 2020). Nonetheless, as digital media enable 'new opportunities for non-elite actors to mobilise and enter the news making process' (Chadwick 2017: 6), they ferment ad hoc publics (Bruns and Burgess 2015) and further erode the public sphere values of journalism.

We know that online networks can be a breeding ground for radicalisation and polarisation (Baumann et al. 2020; Resende et al. 2019) and that microtargeted advertising allows political actors to produce selective information for different cohorts in a society, often based on ideas about affective attitudes (Ali et al. 2019; O'Connor and Weatherall 2019). For example, prior to the Brexit referendum, the Leave campaign's online adverts targeted specific interests including immigration ('5.23 million more migrants moving to the UK') and animal rights ('If we stay in the EU, we will be powerless to increase protection for polar bears') (Worall 2018). As noted in Chapter 2, Russian disinformation has sought to amplify polarisation by targeting left-leaning activists with messages vilifying conservatives and vice versa (O'Connor and Weatherall 2019). Quite apart from any impact on election outcomes, these revelations intensify the core issue of how to place trust in the digital environment.

The philosopher Onora O'Neill (2017) makes an influential distinction between trustworthiness and trust. While reports of declining public trust in authorities place emphasis on the public's apparent lack of faith in experts and institutions, the concept of trustworthiness places emphasis on whether those experts and institutions merit public trust in the first place. As Newton (2001) argues, social and political trust are rooted in people's experience of the social and political world. Social trust is expressed by people who feel they are generally surrounded by trustworthy people, and political trust is expressed by people who feel that their political system and its politicians generally perform satisfactorily. Following O'Neill's view, institutions – whether platforms, political parties, or media outlets – should not aim to increase public trust, but to demonstrate their trustworthiness through honesty, competence, and reliability. Historically, the response to concerns about the trustworthiness of experts has been the regulation of professions and the imposition of standards. This suggests that we need a way to define and implement standards for the digital age.

In the early years of the web, many scholars recognised that new technologies presented 'the contours of historically new conditions for the public sphere' (Dahlgren 1991: 14). The mistake was to assume that these conditions would be realised by themselves. It is also a mistake, we argue, to disregard the democratic potential of digital media. Rather than bemoan the decline of traditional gatekeepers, Weinberger (2011) argues that digital media open up new ways to think about how truth is conferred and contested. He observes that the processes of selecting and framing content in traditional media are made more explicit and transparent in online communication such that 'networked knowledge brings us closer to the truth about knowledge' (Weinberger 2011: 196). For example, the editorial process behind the creation of an authoritative book or encyclopaedia – or, indeed, a news article – remains hidden from readers. In contrast, the model of cooperative production on Wikipedia exposes the complex and contested process of compiling information and determining its authority. Among the world's most popular websites, Wikipedia stands out as the only non-commercial entity. Although Wikipedia isn't perfect, it does, as Zuckerman (2019) argues, offer a model of what public media could look like in the online environment.

The question then is how to design platforms that are conducive to civil participation and trustworthy communication while providing accountability for users. As noted in the preceding chapters, emerging research offers promising insights on designing effective corrections to false information or inoculations that preempt disinformation strategies (Pennycook et al. 2020; Tully et al. 2020). This work is largely conceived as a reaction to problem content, but the platforms of the future could build in structures that advance trust and civil participation. Of course, technology alone cannot render a society more inclusive or democratic in character and it cannot reverse the polarisation trends described above. As Habermas 1996: 219) argues, 'only in an egalitarian public of citizens that has emerged from the confines of class and thrown off the millennia old shackles of social stratification and exploitation can the potential of an unleashed cultural pluralism fully develop'. At a more fundamental level, the core issue of trust requires finding ways to reinvigorate democracy. In this context, Bennett and Livingstone (2018) argue that fact-checking and media literacy initiatives are unlikely to be sufficient as they do little to repair political institutions and democratic values. Similarly, Chambers (2020: 2) argues that 'slowing down, debunking, and exposing fake news will only have an impact if citizens care about, and make efforts to acquire, the truth'. If the health of democracy depends on the will of citizens to base their political judgements on evidence (Persily 2017) and on political institutions ability to demonstrate trustworthiness through honesty, competence, and reliability (O'Neill 2017), then we suggest that innovations in deliberative democracy may offer a path forward.

Reinvigorating democracy

Democratic societies face profound challenges on many fronts. As noted, the information environment is subject to major disruptions including: a decline in the quality of news and political information; a decline in pluralism as media ownership becomes more concentrated; increased fragmentation and polarisation within populations; increased relativism in public debate; and increased inequalities in political knowledge (Bennett and Pfetsch 2018; Van Aelst et al. 2017). The hollowing out of democracy was presciently observed by the late political scientist Peter Mair (2013) who argued that democracy is being steadily stripped of its popular component – the demos – and mechanisms for meaningful citizen engagement (Mair 2013). Regarding the diagnosis of a post-truth culture, Farkas and Schou (2019: 154) similarly conclude that 'democracy does not need more truth but more politics and popular rule'. From this perspective, finding ways to reinvigorate democracy and public participation is key to addressing the range of ills described above.

As noted, deliberative theories of democracy propose that communication and cooperation among citizens are essential for well-informed and legitimate public decision-making (Goodin and Dryzek 2006; Habermas 1996). Deliberative mini-publics (DMPs), public inquiries, town hall meetings, online consultations, and informal discussions – all have their place in a modern, innovating democracy. We focus here on DMPs although we stress that there is neither a magic bullet nor one ideal way in which to engage with citizens.

Nonetheless, deliberative 'mini-publics' are an important democratic innovation that supports the participation of citizens in policy making (Goodin and Dryzek 2006). As Cuarto et al. (2020) point out, a decade ago we had not imagined that a group of 100 French citizens could deliberate on how to reach climate change targets, or that a similar number of Irish citizens could deliberate on changes to controversial abortion laws. Yet they did, and demonstrated that disinformation and attacks on evidence and expertise can be overcome.

Put simply, mini-publics bring together a group of randomly selected citizens in face-to-face settings where they are presented with relevant information and, with the support of trained moderators, follow procedures for deliberating the issues and arriving at a decision or policy recommendation. As outlined below, there is growing evidence that citizens in these settings are competent and respectful debaters who are capable of arriving at evidence-based solutions to policy problems.

Mini publics can contribute to a more informed public sphere in many ways. They can improve the information environment by providing information resources including factual information and knowledge; by fostering citizens' analytical capacities including relative and critical thinking; and by developing the communication skills to frame arguments around a common good and to engage in discussion with others (Suiter et al. 2020). The recommendations and conclusions of a mini public may also act as a heuristic for other citizens' understanding of an issue. Mini-public participants who have engaged with and evaluated the evidence may be recognised as 'enlightened peers' with access to correct information (Fournier 2011: 127) such that their conclusions are considered non-partisan and less biased (Már and Gastil 2020).

While deliberation in mini publics aims to create an 'enlightened understanding' (Dahl 1991: 112), it is not only in respect to knowledge and evidence. It also includes the development of emotional and emphatic capacities. In particular, empathy is necessary to consider how collective decisions impact the full demos and it is empathy that gives legitimacy to collective decisions (Morrell 2010) and reduces the distance between polarised citizens by promoting inclusiveness and strengthening mutual respect and reciprocity (Goodin 2003; Morrell 2010). For example, Muradova (2020) finds that mini public deliberation encourages participants to take on the perspective of others including those of opposite points of view. Studies in Ireland found that exposing members of the public to mini public statements increased their empathy for the other side of the policy debate (Suiter et al. 2020). This is reflective of earlier research which found that increasing awareness of the viewpoints of the other side can increase tolerance (Mutz 2002). There is hope therefore that the interpersonal contact across racial, ethnic, and demographic characteristics has the potential to reduce prejudicial attitudes and increase perspective taking (Pettigrew and Tropp 2011). Relatedly, facilitated deliberation among heterogeneous groups of citizens appears to mitigate against the cognitive errors and biases described in Chapter 4. For example, framing effects appear to lose their efficacy in the face of discussion in heterogeneous groups where different perspectives are foregrounded (Druckman 2004). Similarly, Strandberg et al. (2019) found that polarisation could be avoided in groups with deliberative norms whereas free discussion without rules tends towards group polarisation.

The practice of deliberative democracy is steadily gaining momentum. Influential cases include: Deliberative Polls (Fishkin 2009); the Irish Constitutional Convention (Suiter et al. 2016): the Irish Citizens' Assembly (Farrell et al. 2018); and the Citizens' Initiative Review in Oregon (Gastil et al. 2018). These real-world initiatives have created a Habermasian communication process featuring moderated discussions among diverse groups of citizens as well as numerous submissions from experts and public stakeholders. While the number of citizens participating in deliberation may be low (approximately 100), the wider public gains an understanding of what their peers concluded following a period of deliberation (Gastil et al. 2014; Warren and Gastil 2015). For example, evidence from the Irish experience indicates that the recommendations put forward by the deliberating citizens were widely disseminated (Elkink et al. 2020; Suiter and Reidy 2020). Importantly, studies of subsequent referendums found that voters who were aware of the mini-public had higher levels of accurate knowledge about the referendum topic and were more likely to vote in line with the mini public's recommendations (ibid). Returning to disinformation, it is, of course, very difficult for bad actors to infiltrate mini publics. Indeed, there is a growing hope that such deliberative bodies, if properly moderated and facilitated, can help ameliorate the impact of disinformation (Curato et al. 2017) and hinder the attempts of bad actors to ferment polarisation.

The big question, of course, is how to expand the normative conditions of mini-publics. Within the deliberation literature, there is growing focus on embedding deliberation 'downstream' in the policy process. This focus on mitigating power asymmetries in democratic politics is in line with Habermas' work on communicative ethics in the public sphere. For example, Boswell (2016) advocates various institutional innovations as well as emerging governing practices including structured partnerships, which guarantee lesser-resourced actors informal access, and co-production, including citizen participation in the provision of public services. These kinds of innovations also lie behind recent OECD (2020) efforts to encourage innovative citizen participation in policymaking. The key insight is that implementing deliberative principles within the public sphere, in classrooms and in civic education initiatives such as media literacy, leads to mutual respect (Hanson and Howe 2011) and addresses the epistemic issues of democracy by recognising the moral and social differences that exist within society particularly around controversial issues that often give opportunities to bad actors to produce disinformation.

To date, deliberative assemblies have largely taken place in face-to-face environments. It is only in the Covid-19 world of 2020 that formal assemblies have migrated online including, for example, the French and Scottish deliberative assemblies on climate change and the Irish assembly on gender equality. There is some evidence that the outcomes of online deliberation may not differ from their offline counterparts as long as the discussion is synchronistic, moderated by humans, and follows strict rules for civility (Gronlund et al. 2009; Strandberg et al. 2019). In contrast, deliberation without moderation is likely to become polarised (Strandberg and Grönlund 2018). Promisingly, participating in deliberation has been found to generate more empathetic feelings and understanding toward others (Morrell 2010; Grönlund et al. 2017; Muradova 2020). However, this work has not yet been conducted in an online environment and it is too early to tell if the same benefits translate in a digital context where face-to-face cues are lost.

Conclusion

Clearly, there is much work to be done to advance the practice of deliberative democracy and we do not suggest it is a ready-made remedy for all the problems outlined in this book. Nor do we suggest that deliberative norms could replace the range of disinformation countermeasures outlined in Chapter 5. Online disinformation is a complex problem with multiple, overlapping causes and no easy solutions. It requires short-term responses such as greater access to platform data, fact-checking, and media literacy as well as long-term responses such as regulating or co-regulating the platforms and devising norms and standards that support truth, trust, and accountability in both offline and online contexts. After all, disinformation and the erosion of democratic values does not occur in an online vacuum. Over the long term, we suggest embedding deliberative norms in offline and online contexts may go some way to ameliorating the problems described in this book. But the context of that participation matters. Citizens need to be offered a space in which they can engage with a diverse group, where changing one's mind is encouraged and where consideration of evidence and good judgement are virtues. As Chambers (2018: 36) puts it, citizens 'are good problem solvers even if we are poor solitary truth seekers'. We thus need to be able to make better decisions together. To return to Habermas, if we facilitate deliberative norms through governance, accountability mechanisms, and design structures, perhaps we can find the kind of communicative action that supports mutual understanding and cooperation.

References

Ali M, Sapiezynski P, Korolova A et al. (2019) Ad delivery algorithms: the hidden arbiters of political messaging. *arXiv:1912.04255 [cs]*. Available at: http://arxiv.org/abs/1912.04255.

Arendt H (2006) *Between Past and Future: Eight Exercises in Political Thought*. New York: Penguin Books.

Baumann F, Lorenz-Spreen P, Sokolov IM et al. (2020) Modeling echo chambers and polarization dynamics in social networks. *Physical Review Letters* 124(4). DOI: 10.1103/PhysRevLett.124.048301.

Benkler Y (2006) *The Wealth of Networks: How Social Production Transforms Markets and Freedom*. New Haven: Yale University Press.

Benkler Y, Faris R and Roberts H (2018) *Network Propaganda: Manipulation, Disinformation, and Radicalization in American Politics*. New York: Oxford University Press.

Bennett WL and Livingston S (2018) The disinformation order: disruptive communication and the decline of democratic institutions. *European Journal of Communication* 33(2): 122–139. DOI: 10.1177/0267323118760317.

Bennett WL and Pfetsch B (2018) Rethinking political communication in a time of disrupted public spheres. *Journal of Communication* 68(2): 243–253. DOI: 10.1093/joc/jqx017.

Berners-Lee T (2018) One small step for the web... In: *Medium*. Available at: https://medium.com/@timberners_lee/one-small-step-for-the-web-87f92217d085.

Boswell J (2016) Deliberating downstream: countering democratic distortions in the policy process. *Perspectives on Politics* 14(3): 724–737. DOI: 10.1017/S1537592716001146.

Bruns A and Burgess J (n.d.) Twitter hashtags from ad hoc to calculated publics. In: Rambukkana N (ed.) *Hashtag Publics: The Power and Politics of Discursive Networks*. New York: Peter Lang, pp. 13–28.

Chadwick A (2017) *The Hybrid Media System: Politics and Power*. Second edition. New York: Oxford University Press.

Chambers S (2020) Truth, deliberative democracy, and the virtues of accuracy: is fake news destroying the public sphere? *Political Studies*. DOI: 10.1177/0032321719890811.

Curato N, Dryzek JS, Ercan SA et al. (2017) Twelve key findings in deliberative democracy research. *Daedalus* 146(3): 28–38. DOI: 10.1162/DAED_a_00444.

Curato N, Farrell, DM, Geißel, B, Gronlund, K, Mockler, P, Pilet, JB et al. (2020) *Deliberative Mini-Publics: Core Design Features*. Cambridge: Policy Press.

Curran J (1996) Mass media and democracy revisited. In: Curran J and Gurevitch M (eds) *Mass Media and Society*. Second edition. London: Arnold, pp. 81–119.

D'Ancona M (2017) *Post Truth: The New War on Truth and How to Fight Back*. London: Ebury Press.

Dahl RA (1991) *Democracy and Its Critics*. 12. print. New Haven: Yale Univ. Press.

Dahlgren PM (n.d.) Introduction. In: Dahlgren PM and Sparks C (eds) *Communication and Citizenship: Journalism and the Public Sphere*. London: Routledge, pp. 1–24.

Dede C (2008) A seismic shift in epistemology. *EDUCAUSE Review* 43(3): 80–81.

Druckman JN (2004) Political preference formation: competition, deliberation, and the (ir)relevance of framing effects. *American Political Science Review* 98(4): 671–686. DOI: 10.1017/S0003055404041413.

Elkink JA, Farrell DM, Marien S et al. (2020) The death of conservative Ireland? The 2018 abortion referendum. *Electoral Studies* 65: 102142. DOI: 10.1016/j.electstud.2020.102142.

Farkas J and Schou J (2019) *Post-Truth, Fake News and Democracy: Mapping the Politics of Falsehood*. Abingdon: Routledge.

Finlayson L (2019) What to do with post-truth. *Nordic Wittgenstein Review*: 63–79. DOI: 10.15845/nwr.v8i0.3502.

Fournier P (ed.) (2011) *When Citizens Decide: Lessons from Citizen Assemblies on Electoral Reform*. New York: Oxford University Press.

Gastil J, Richards RC and Knobloch K (2014) Vicarious deliberation: how the Oregon citizens' initiative review influenced deliberation in mass elections. *International Journal of Communication* 8: 62–89.

Goodin RE (2003) *Reflective Democracy*. Oxford: Oxford University Press.

Goodin RE and Dryzek JS (2006) Deliberative impacts: the macro-political uptake of mini-publics. *Politics & Society* 34(2): 219–244. DOI: 10.1177/0032329206288152.

Grönlund K, Strandberg K and Himmelroos S (2017) The challenge of deliberative democracy online – a comparison of face-to-face and virtual experiments in citizen deliberation. *Information Polity* 14(3): 187–201.

Habermas J (1962) *The Structural Transformation of the Public Sphere: An Inquiry into a Category of Bourgeois Society*. Cambridge, MA: The MIT Press.

Habermas J (1996) *Between Facts and Norms: Contributions to a Discourse Theory of Law and Democracy*. Cambridge, MA: MIT Press.

Hanitzsch T, Van Dalen A and Steindl N (2018) Caught in the nexus: a comparative and longitudinal analysis of public trust in the press. *The International Journal of Press/Politics* 23(1): 3–23. DOI: 10.1177/1940161217740695.

Hanson J and Howe K (2011) The potential for deliberative democratic civic education. *Democracy and Education* 19(2): 3.

Hopmann DN, Shehata A and Strömbäck J (2015) Contagious media effects: how media use and exposure to game-framed news influence media trust. *Mass Communication and Society* 18(6): 776–798. DOI: 10.1080/15205436.2015.1022190.

Hyvönen A-E (2018) Careless speech: conceptualizing post-truth politics. *New Perspectives* 26(3): 31–55.

Jenkins H (2006) *Convergence Culture: Where Old and New Media Collide*. New York: New York University Press.

Jones DA (2004) Why Americans don't trust the media: a preliminary analysis. *Harvard International Journal of Press/Politics* 9(2): 60–75. DOI: 10.1177/1081180X04263461.

Keen A (2007) *The Cult of the Amateur: How Today's Internet Is Killing Our Culture*. First edition. New York: Doubleday/Currency.

Kellner D (2016) *American Nightmare*. Rotterdam: SensePublishers. DOI: 10.1007/978-94-6300-788-7.

Mair P (2013) *Ruling the Void: The Hollowing of Western Democracy*. London: Verso.

Már K and Gastil J (2020) Tracing the boundaries of motivated reasoning: how deliberative minipublics can improve voter knowledge. *Political Psychology* 41(1): 107–127. DOI: 10.1111/pops.12591.

Morrell ME (2010) *Empathy and Democracy: Feeling, Thinking, and Deliberation*. University Park, PA: Pennsylvania State University Press.

Muradova L (2020) Seeing the other side? Perspective-taking and reflective political judgements in interpersonal deliberation. *Political Studies*. DOI: 10.1177/0032321720916605.

Newman N, Fletcher R, Kalogeropoulos A et al. (2019) *Reuters Institute Digital News Report 2019*. Oxford: Reuters Institute for the Study of Journalism.

Newton K (2001) Trust, social capital, civil society, and democracy. *International Political Science Review* 22(2): 201–214. DOI: 10.1177/0192512101222004.

O'Connor C and Weatherall JO (2019) *The Misinformation Age: How False Beliefs Spread*. New Haven: Yale University Press.

O'Neill O (n.d.) Intelligent trust in a digital world. *New Perspectives Quarterly* 34(4): 27–31.

OECD (2020) *Innovative Citizen Participation and New Democratic Institutions*. OECD. Available at: www.oecd.org/gov/innovative-citizen-participation-and-new-democratic-institutions-339306da-en.htm.

Pariser E (2012) *The Filter Bubble: What the Internet Is Hiding from You*. London: Penguin Books.

Pennycook G, McPhetres J, Zhang Y et al. (2020) Fighting Covid-19 misinformation on social media: Experimental evidence for a scalable accuracy nudge intervention. Available at: https://psyarxiv.com/uhbk9/.

Persily N (2017) Can democracy survive the internet? *Journal of Democracy* 28(2): 63–76. DOI: 10.1353/jod.2017.0025.

Pettigrew TF and Tropp LR (2011) *When Groups Meet: The Dynamics of Intergroup Contact*. New York: Psychology Press.

Pickard VW (2020) *Democracy Without Journalism?: Confronting the Misinformation Society*. New York: Oxford University Press.

Repucci S (2019) *Freedom and the Media: A Downward Spiral*. Washington, DC: Freedom House.

Resende G, Melo P, and Sousa H et al. (2019) (Mis)Information dissemination in WhatsApp: gathering, analyzing and countermeasures. In: *The World Wide Web Conference on – WWW '19*. San Francisco, CA, USA, 2019, pp. 818–828. ACM Press. DOI: 10.1145/3308558.3313688.

Shirky C (2009) *Here Comes Everybody: The Power of Organizing without Organizations*. New York: Penguin Books.

Strandberg K and Grönlund K (2018) Online deliberation. In: Bächtiger A, Dryzek JS, Mansbridge J et al. (eds) *The Oxford Handbook of Deliberative Democracy.* Oxford: Oxford University Press, pp. 365–377.

Strandberg K, Himmelroos S and Grönlund K (2019) Do discussions in like-minded groups necessarily lead to more extreme opinions? Deliberative democracy and group polarization. *International Political Science Review* 40(1): 41–57. DOI: 10.1177/0192512117692136.

Suiter J and Fletcher R (2020) Polarization and partisanship: key drivers of distrust in media old and new? *European Journal of Communication.* DOI: 10.1177/0267323120903685.

Suiter J and Reidy T (2019) Does deliberation help deliver informed electorates: evidence from Irish Referendum votes. *Representation*: 1–19. DOI: 10.1080/00344893.2019.1704848.

Suiter J, Farrell D and Harris C (2016) The Irish constitutional convention: a case of 'high legitimacy'? In: Reuchamps M and Suiter J (eds) *Constitutional Deliberative Democracy in Europe.* Colchester: ECPR Press.

Suiter J, Muradova L, Gastil J et al. (n.d.) Scaling up deliberation: testing the potential of mini-publics to enhance the deliberative capacity of citizens. *Swiss Political Science Review.*

Sunstein CR (2011) *Going to Extremes: How Like Minds Unite and Divide.* Oxford: Oxford University Press.

Tsfati Y and Ariely G (2014) Individual and contextual correlates of trust in media across 44 countries. *Communication Research* 41(6): 760–782. DOI: 10.1177/0093650213485972.

Tsfati Y and Cohen J (2005) The influence of presumed media influence on democratic legitimacy: the case of Gaza settlers. *Communication Research* 32(6): 794–821. DOI: 10.1177/0093650205281057.

Tully M, Vraga EK and Bode L (2020) Designing and testing news literacy messages for social media. *Mass Communication and Society* 23(1): 22–46. DOI: 10.1080/15205436.2019.1604970.

Vallone RP, Ross L and Lepper MR (1985) The hostile media phenomenon: biased perception and perceptions of media bias in coverage of the Beirut massacre. *Journal of Personality and Social Psychology* 49(3): 577–585. DOI: 10.1037/0022-3514.49.3.577.

Van Aelst P, Strömbäck J, Aalberg T et al. (2017) Political communication in a high-choice media environment: a challenge for democracy? *Annals of the International Communication Association* 41(1): 3–27. DOI: 10.1080/23808985.2017.1288551.

van Zoonen L (2012) i-Pistemology: changing truth claims in popular and political culture. *European Journal of Communication* 27(1): 56–67. DOI: 10.1177/0267323112438808.

Waisbord S (2018) Truth is what happens to news: on journalism, fake news, and post-truth. *Journalism Studies* 19(13): 1866–1878. DOI: 10.1080/1461670X.2018.1492881.

Warren ME and Gastil J (2015) Can deliberative minipublics address the cognitive challenges of democratic citizenship? *The Journal of Politics* 77(2): 562–574. DOI: 10.1086/680078.

Weinberger D (2011) *Too Big to Know: Rethinking Knowledge Now That the Facts Aren't the Facts, Experts Are Everywhere, and the Smartest Person in the Room Is the Room.* New York: Basic Books.

Wong JC and Levin S (2017) Republican candidate charged with assault after 'body-slamming' Guardian reporter. *The Guardian*, 25 May. Available at: www.theguardian.com/us-news/2017/may/24/greg-gianforte-bodyslams-reporter-ben-jacobs-montana.

Worall P (2018) Vote Leave's 'dark' Brexit ads. *Channel 4*, 27 July. Available at: www.channel4.com/news/factcheck/factcheck-vote-leaves-dark-brexit-ads.

Zuckerman E (2019) Building a more honest internet. *Columbia Journalism Review*. Available at: www.cjr.org/special_report/building-honest-internet-public-interest.php.

Index

Printed in the United States
by Baker & Taylor Publisher Services